D1381556

Worship Today

Songs and hymns for the whole church

SPRING HARVEST

Equipping the Church for action

Worship Today

1
A NEW COMMANDMENT
I give unto you,
that you love one another
as I have loved you,
that you love one another
as I have loved you.

By this shall all men know
that you are my disciples,
if you have love one for another.
(Repeat)

Author unknown

2
ABBA FATHER
let me be yours and yours alone.
May my will forever be
ever more your own.
Never let my heart grow cold,
never let me go.
Abba Father, let me be
yours and yours alone.

Dave Bilbrough
Copyright © 1977 Kingsway's Thankyou Music

3
AH LORD GOD
thou hast made the heavens
and the earth by thy great power.
Ah Lord God, thou hast made the heavens
and the earth by thine outstretched arm.

Nothing is too difficult for thee,
nothing is too difficult for thee.
O great and mighty God,
great in counsel and mighty in deed,
nothing, nothing,
absolutely nothing,
nothing is too difficult for thee.

Copyright © Kay Chance

3a   The power of God
Jeremiah 32:17

Ah, Sovereign Lord, you have made the
heavens and the earth by your great power
and outstretched arm.
Nothing is too hard for you.

4
ALL AROUND THE WORLD
there's a new day dawning,
there's a sound coming round,
there's a new song rising up,
ah, it's a new day!
Everywhere you go you can hear this story,
there's a power coming down,
there's a glimpse of glory now,
ah, it's a new day!

There's a sound of praise,
there's a sound of war;
lift the banner high, let the Lion roar.
Can you hear the sound in the tops of the trees?
Heaven's armies come! Crush the enemy!

Let the lame run, let the blind see!
Let your power come, set the captives free!
Let the lost return to the Lover of our souls,
Let the prodigal find the way back home.

Lift your hands before the King,
the sovereign Ruler of the earth;
let the nations come to him,
Let the cry of hearts be heard:

Revive us! Revive us! Revive us again! (Repeat)

Paul Oakley
Copyright © 1997 Kingsway's Thankyou Music

5
ALL HAIL KING JESUS
All hail Emmanuel!
King of kings, Lord of lords,
bright morning star.

And throughout eternity I'll sing your praises,
and I'll reign with you throughout eternity.

Dave Moody. Copyright © 1984
Dayspring/Word Music admin. by CopyCare

6
ALL HAIL THE LAMB
enthroned on high;
his praise shall be our battle cry.
He reigns victorious, forever glorious,
his name is Jesus, he is the Lord.

Dave Bilbrough
Copyright © 1987 Kingsway's Thankyou Music

7

ALL HEAVEN DECLARES

the glory of the risen Lord.
Who can compare
with the beauty of the Lord?
Forever he will be
the Lamb upon the throne.
I gladly bow the knee
and worship him alone.

I will proclaim
the glory of the risen Lord,
who once was slain
to reconcile man to God.
Forever you will be
the Lamb upon the throne.
I gladly bow the knee
and worship you alone.

Noel & Tricia Richards
Copyright © 1987 Kingsway's Thankyou Music

8

ALL I ONCE HELD DEAR

built my life upon,
all this world reveres and wars to own;
all I once thought gain I have counted loss;
spent and worthless now, compared to this.

Knowing you, Jesus, knowing you,
there is no greater thing:
you're my all, you're the best,
you're my joy, my righteousness;
and I love you, Lord.

Now my heart's desire is to know you more,
to be found in you and known as yours;
to possess by faith what I could not earn –
all-surpassing gift of righteousness.

Oh, to know the power of your risen life,
and to know you in your sufferings;
to become like you in your death, my Lord,
so with you to live and never die!

Graham Kendrick
Copyright © 1993 Make Way Music

8a   Suffering with Christ
Philippians 3:10–11

I want to know Christ and the power of his
resurrection and the fellowship of sharing in
his sufferings, becoming like him in his death,
and so, somehow, to attain to the resurrection
from the dead.

9

ALL MY DAYS

I will sing this song of gladness,
give my praise to the Fountain of delights;
for in my helplessness you heard my cry,
and waves of mercy poured down on my life.

I will trust in the cross of my Redeemer,
I will sing of the blood that never fails,
of sins forgiven, of conscience cleansed,
of death defeated and life without end.

Beautiful Saviour, wonderful Counsellor,
clothed in majesty, Lord of history,
you're the way, the truth, the life.
Star of the morning, glorious in holiness,
you're the risen One, heaven's champion,
and you reign, you reign over all!

I long to be where the praise is never-ending,
yearn to dwell where the glory never fades,
where countless worshippers will share one song,
and cries of 'worthy' will honour the Lamb!

Stuart Townend
Copyright © 1998 Kingsway's Thankyou Music

10

ALL THAT I AM

I lay before you;
all I possess, Lord, I confess is nothing without you.
Saviour and King, I now enthrone you;
take my life, my living sacrifice to you.

Lord, be the strength within my weakness;
be the supply in every need,
that I may prove your promises to me,
faithful and true in word and deed.

Into your hands I place the future;
the past is nailed to Calvary,
that I may live in resurrection power,
no longer I but Christ in me.

James Wright
Copyright © 1994 Kingsway's Thankyou Music

11

ALL OVER THE WORLD

the Spirit is moving,
all over the world as the prophet said it would be;
all over the world there's a mighty revelation
of the glory of the Lord, as the waters cover the sea.

All over his church God's Spirit is moving,
all over his church as the prophet said it would be;
all over his church there's a mighty revelation
of the glory of the Lord, as the waters cover the sea.

Right here in this place the Spirit is moving,
right here in this place
as the prophet said it would be;
right here in this place there's a mighty revelation
of the glory of the Lord,
as the waters cover the sea.

12
ALLELUIA, ALLELUIA
give thanks to the risen Lord,
alleluia, alleluia, give praise to his name.

Jesus is Lord of all the earth,
he is the King of creation.

Spread the good news o'er all the earth,
Jesus has died and has risen.

We have been crucified with Christ,
now we shall live forever.

God has proclaimed the just reward,
life for all men, alleluia!

Come let us praise the living God,
joyfully sing to our Saviour.

13
ALMIGHTY GOD, MY REDEEMER
my hiding place, my safe refuge;
no other name like Jesus,
no power can stand against you.
My feet are planted on this rock,
and I will not be shaken;
my hope it comes from you alone,
my Lord and my salvation.

Your praise is always on my lips,
your word is living in my heart,
and I will praise you with a new song:
my soul will bless you, Lord.
You fill my life with greater joy;
yes, I delight myself in you,
and I will praise you with a new song:
my soul will bless you, Lord.

When I am weak, you make me strong;
when I'm poor, I know I'm rich,
for in the power of your name
all things are possible. (x4)

14
ALMIGHTY GOD, WE BRING YOU PRAISE
for your Son, the Word of God,
by whose power the world was made,
by whose blood we are redeemed.
Morning Star, the Father's glory,
we now worship and adore you.
In our hearts your light has risen;
Jesus, Lord, we worship you.

15
AMAZING GRACE
how sweet the sound
that saved a wretch like me;
I once was lost, but now am found,
was blind, but now I see.

'Twas grace that taught my heart to fear,
and grace my fears relieved;
how precious did that grace appear,
the hour I first believed!

Through many dangers, toils and snares
I have already come;
'tis grace that brought me safe thus far,
and grace will lead me home.

The Lord has promised good to me,
his word my hope secures;
he will my shield and portion be
as long as life endures.

Yes, when this heart and flesh shall fail,
and mortal life shall cease,
I shall possess within the veil
a life of joy and peace.

When we've been there a thousand years,
bright shining as the sun,
we've no less days to sing God's praise
than when we first begun.

16
AN ARMY OF ORDINARY PEOPLE
a kingdom where love is the key,
a city, a light to the nations,
heirs to the promise are we.
A people whose life is in Jesus,
a nation together we stand.
Only through grace are we worthy,
inheritors of the land.

continued over...

A new day is dawning,
a new age to come,
when the children of promise
shall flow together as one.
A truth long neglected,
but the time has now come
when the children of promise
shall flow together as one.

A people without recognition,
but with him a destiny sealed,
called to a heavenly vision,
his purpose shall be fulfilled.
Come, let us stand strong together,
abandon ourselves to the King,
his love shall be ours forever,
this victory song we shall sing.

Dave Bilbrough
Copyright © 1983 Kingsway's Thankyou Music

17
AND CAN IT BE
that I should gain
an interest in the Saviour's blood?
Died he for me, who caused his pain;
for me, who him to death pursued?
Amazing love! how can it be
that thou, my God, shouldst die for me?

'Tis mystery all! The Immortal dies,
who can explore his strange design?
In vain the first-born seraph tries
to sound the depths of love divine!
'Tis mercy all! let earth adore;
let angel minds inquire no more.

He left his Father's throne above –
so free, so infinite his grace –
emptied himself of all but love,
and bled for Adam's helpless race.
'Tis mercy all, immense and free;
for, O my God, it found out me.

Long my imprisoned spirit lay
fast bound in sin and nature's night;
thine eye diffused a quickening ray;
I woke, the dungeon flamed with light.
My chains fell off, my heart was free;
I rose, went forth, and followed thee.

No condemnation now I dread;
Jesus, and all in him, is mine!
Alive in him, my living head,
and clothed in righteousness divine,
bold I approach the eternal throne,
and claim the crown, through Christ my own.

Charles Wesley

18
AND HE SHALL REIGN FOREVER,
his throne and crown shall ever endure.
And he shall reign forever,
and we shall reign with him.

What a vision filled my eyes,
one like a Son of Man.
Coming with the clouds of heaven
he approached an awesome throne.

He was given sovereign power, glory and authority.
Every nation, tribe and tongue
worshipped him on bended knee.

On the throne forever,
see the Lamb who once was slain.
Wounds of sacrificial love forever shall remain.

Graham Kendrick
Copyright © 1991 Make Way Music

19
ARE WE THE PEOPLE
who will see God's kingdom come,
when he is known in every nation?
One thing is certain, we are closer than before;
keep moving on, last generation.

These are the days for harvest,
to gather in the lost;
let those who live in darkness
hear the message of the cross.

We'll go where God is sending,
we'll do what he commands;
these years that he has waited
could be coming to an end.

Noel & Tricia Richards
Copyright © 1996 Kingsway's Thankyou Music

20
AS FOR ME AND MY HOUSE,
as for me and my family,
as for me and my children,
we will serve the Lord.
(Repeat)

In this family we're gonna do things properly,
read God's word every day
and then we'll try to pray;
although we get it wrong, we will still carry on,
make Jesus number one in this place.

... in this place we're gonna say grace.

Jim Bailey
Copyright © Kingsway's Thankyou Music

6

20a The commandments are passed on
Deuteronomy 6:6-7

These commandments that I give you
today are to be upon your hearts.
Impress them on your children.
Talk about them when you sit at home and
when you walk along the road, when you lie
down and when you get up.

21
AS SURE AS GOLD IS PRECIOUS

and the honey sweet,
so you love this city and you love these streets.
Every child out playing by their own front door;
every baby laying on the bedroom floor.

Every dreamer dreaming in her dead-end job;
every driver driving through the rush hour mob.
I feel it in my spirit, feel it in my bones
you're going to send revival,
        bring them all back home.

I can hear that thunder in the distance
like a train on the edge of town;
I can feel the brooding of your Spirit,
'lay your burdens down,
lay your burdens down.'

From the preacher preaching when the well is dry
to the lost soul reaching for a higher high.
From the young man working
        through his hopes and fears
to the widow walking through the veil of tears.

Every man and woman, every old and young;
every father's daughter, every mother's son.
I feel it in my spirit, feel it in my bones
you're going to send revival,
        bring them all back home.

I can hear...

Revive us, revive us, revive us with your fire!

22
AS THE DEER

pants for the water
so my soul longs after you.
You alone are my heart's desire
and I long to worship you.

You alone are my strength, my shield,
to you alone may my spirit yield.
You alone are my heart's desire
and I long to worship you.

I want you more than gold or silver,
only you can satisfy.
You alone are the real joy-giver
and the apple of my eye.

You're my friend and you are my brother,
even though you are a king.
I love you more than any other,
so much more than anything.

23
AS WATER TO THE THIRSTY

as beauty to the eyes,
as strength that follows weakness,
as truth instead of lies;
as songtime and springtime
and summertime to be,
so is my Lord, my living Lord,
so is my Lord to me.

Like calm in place of clamour,
like peace that follows pain,
like meeting after parting,
like sunshine after rain;
like moonlight and starlight
and sunlight on the sea,
so is my Lord, my living Lord,
so is my Lord to me.

As sleep that follows fever,
as gold instead of grey,
as freedom after bondage,
as sunrise to the day;
as home to the traveller
and all he longs to see,
so is my Lord, my living Lord,
so is my Lord to me.

24
AS WE ARE GATHERED

Jesus is here; one with each other, Jesus is here.
Joined by the Spirit, washed in the blood,
part of the body, the church of God.
As we are gathered Jesus is here,
one with each other, Jesus is here.

25

AS WE SEEK

your face, may we know your heart,
feel your presence, acceptance,
as we seek your face.

Move among us now,
come reveal your power,
show your presence, acceptance,
move among us now.

At your feet we fall,
Sovereign Lord,
we cry 'holy, holy',
at your feet we fall.

Dave Bilbrough
Copyright © 1990 Kingsway's Thankyou Music

26

ASCRIBE GREATNESS

to our God the Rock,
his work is perfect and all his ways are just.
Ascribe greatness to our God, the Rock,
his work is perfect and all his ways are just.

A God of faithfulness and without injustice,
good and upright is he;
a God of faithfulness and without injustice,
good and upright is he.

P West, M L Locke and M Kirkbride. Copyright © 1979
M Kirkbride Barthow & M L King/Adm. by Integrity's Hosanna! Music
Adm. by Kingsway's Thankyou Music

27

AT THE FOOT OF THE CROSS

I can hardly take it in,
that the King of all creation
was dying for my sin.
And the pain and agony,
and the thorns that pierced your head,
and the hardness of my sinful heart
that left you there for dead.

And O what mercy I have found
at the cross of Calvary;
I will never know your loneliness,
all on account of me.
And I will bow my knee before your throne,
'cause your love has set me free;
and I will give my life to you, dear Lord,
and praise your majesty,
and praise your majesty.

Derek Bond
Copyright © 1992 Sovereign Music UK

28

AT THE NAME OF JESUS

every knee shall bow,
every tongue confess him
King of glory now;
'Tis the Father's pleasure
we should call him Lord,
who from the beginning
was the mighty Word.

Humbled for a season,
to receive a name
from the lips of sinners
unto whom he came;
faithfully he bore it
spotless to the last,
brought it back victorious,
when from death he passed.

Bore it up triumphant
with its human light,
through all ranks of creatures
to the central height,
to the throne of Godhead,
to the Father's breast,
filled it with the glory
of that perfect rest.

In your hearts enthrone him;
there let him subdue
all that is not holy,
all that is not true;
crown him as your Captain
in temptation's hour,
let his will enfold you
in its light and power.

Brothers, this Lord Jesus shall return again,
with his Father's glory,
with his angel-train;
for all wreaths of empire
meet upon his brow,
and our hearts confess him
King of glory now.

Caroline Maria Noel (1817-77)

29

AT YOUR FEET WE FALL

mighty risen Lord,
as we come before your throne to worship you.
By your Spirit's power you now draw our hearts,
and we hear your voice in triumph ringing clear.

I am he that liveth, that liveth and was dead,
behold I am alive forever more.

8

There we see you stand, mighty risen Lord,
clothed in garments pure and holy, shining bright.
Eyes of flashing fire, feet like burnished bronze,
and the sound of many waters is your voice.

Like the shining sun in its noonday strength,
we now see the glory of your wondrous face.
Once that face was marred, but now you're glorified,
and your words like a two-edged sword
    have mighty power.

David Fellingham
Copyright © 1982 Kingsway's Thankyou Music

30

BE BOLD, BE STRONG

for the Lord your God is with you.
(Repeat)

I am not afraid,
I am not dismayed,
because I'm walking in faith and victory,
come on and walk in faith and victory,
for the Lord your God is with you.

Morris Chapman
Copyright © 1983 Word Music admin by CopyCare

30a God will be with you
Joshua 1:9

Have I not commanded you?
Be strong and courageous.
Do not be terrified; do not be discouraged,
for the Lord your God will be with you
wherever you go.

31

BE FREE IN THE LOVE OF GOD

let his Spirit flow within you.
Be free in the love of God, let it fill your soul.
Be free in the love of God,
celebrate his name with dancing.
Be free in the love of God,
he has made us whole.

For his purpose he has called us,
in his hands he will uphold us.
He will keep us and sustain us
in the Father's love.

God is gracious, he will lead us
through his power at work within us.
Spirit guide us, and unite us
in the Father's love.

Dave Bilbrough
Copyright © 1991 Kingsway's Thankyou Music.

31a Jesus is exalted
Philippians 2:5-11

Your attitude should be the same as that of
Christ Jesus:

Who, being in very nature God,
    did not consider equality with God
        something to be grasped,
but made himself nothing,
    taking the very nature of a servant,
    being made in human likeness.
And being found in appearance as a man,
    he humbled himself and became obedient
    to death – even death on a cross!

Therefore God exalted him to the highest
    place and gave him the name that is
    above every name, that at the name
    of Jesus every knee should bow,
in heaven and on earth and under the earth,
and every tongue confess that Jesus Christ
    is Lord, to the glory of God the Father.

32

BE STILL AND KNOW THAT I AM GOD

I will be glorified and praised in all the earth.
For my great name I will be found,
and I can never be resisted, never be undone;
I'm never lacking power to glorify my Son.
The gates of hell are falling
and the church is coming forth,
my name will be exalted in the earth.

Be still and know that I am God;
I have poured out my Holy Spirit like a flood.
The land that cries for holy rain
shall be inheriting her promises
and dancing like a child;
a holy monsoon deluge
shall bless the barren heights,
and those who sat in silence
shall speak up and shall be heard:
my name will be exalted in the earth.

Be still and know that I am God;
my Son has asked me for the nations of the world.
His sprinkled blood has made a way for all
the multitudes of India and Africa to come;
the Middle East will find its peace through
Jesus Christ my Son.
From London down to Cape Town,
from LA to Beijing,
my Son shall reign the undisputed King!

Lex Loizides
Copyright © 1995 Kingsway's Thankyou Music.

33

BE STILL AND KNOW THAT I AM GOD,
(Repeat x2)

I am the Lord that healeth thee...

In thee, O Lord, do I put my trust...

Author unknown.

33a Be still
Psalm 46:10

'Be still, and know that I am God;
I will be exalted among the nations,
I will be exalted in the earth.'

34

BE STILL, FOR THE PRESENCE
of the Lord, the holy One is here;
come bow before him now
with reverence and fear.
In him no sin is found, we stand on holy ground.
Be still, for the presence of the Lord,
the holy One is here.

Be still, for the glory of the Lord
is shining all around;
he burns with holy fire,
with splendour he is crowned.
How awesome is the sight,
our radiant King of light!
Be still, for the glory of the Lord
is shining all around.

Be still, for the power of the Lord
is moving in this place;
he comes to cleanse and heal, to minister his grace.
No work too hard for him,
in faith receive from him.
Be still, for the power of the Lord
is moving in this place.

David J Evans
Copyright © 1986 Kingsway's Thankyou Music

35

BE THOU MY VISION
O Lord of my heart.
Nought be all else to me, save that thou art.
Thou my best thought in the day and the night,
waking or sleeping, thy presence my light.

Be thou my wisdom, be thou my true word,
I ever with thee, and thou with me, Lord.
Thou my great Father and I thy true son,
thou in me dwelling, and I with thee one.

Be thou my breastplate, my sword for the fight,
be thou my armour and be thou my might.
Be my soul's shelter and thou my high tower:
raise thou me heavenwards, O power of my power.

Riches I need not, nor man's empty praise:
thou my inheritance now and always.
Thou and thou only, the first in my heart,
high King of heaven, my treasure thou art.

O high King of heaven, when battle is done
grant heaven's joy to me, bright heaven's sun.
Christ of my own heart, whatever befall,
still be my vision, thou ruler of all.

Tr. Mary E. Byrne & Eleanor H. Hull.

36

BEAUTIFUL LORD
wonderful Saviour,
I know for sure, all of my days
are held in your hand, crafted into your perfect plan.
You gently call me into your presence,
guiding me by your Holy Spirit.
Teach me, dear Lord,
to live all of my life through your eyes.

I'm captured by your holy calling, set me apart,
I know you're drawing me to yourself;
lead me, Lord, I pray.
Take me, mould me, use me, fill me;
I give my life to the potter's hand.
Call me, guide me, lead me, walk beside me;
I give my life to the potter's hand.

Darlene Zschech. Copyright © 1997
Darlene Zschech/Hillsong Publishing/Kingsway's Thankyou Music

37

BEAUTY FOR BROKENNESS,
hope for despair,
Lord, in your suffering world this is our prayer:
bread for the children, justice, joy, peace;
sunrise to sunset, your kingdom increase!

Shelter for fragile lives, cures for their ills,
work for the craftsmen, trade for their skills;
land for the dispossessed, rights for the weak,
voices to plead the cause of those who can't speak.

God of the poor, friend of the weak,
give us compassion we pray:
melt our cold hearts, let tears fall like rain;
come, change our love from a spark to a flame.

Refuge from cruel wars, havens from fear,
cities for sanctuary, freedoms to share;
peace to the killing-fields, scorched earth to green,
Christ for the bitterness, his cross for the pain.

Rest for the ravaged earth, oceans and streams
plundered and poisoned – our future, our dreams.
Lord, end our madness, carelessness, greed;
make us content with the things that we need.

God of the poor...

Lighten our darkness, breathe on this flame
until your justice burns brightly again;
until the nations learn of your ways,
seek your salvation and bring you their praise.

Graham Kendrick
Copyright © 1993 Make Way Music

38
BEFORE THE THRONE

of God above, I have a strong, a perfect plea:
a great high priest, whose name is Love,
who ever lives and pleads for me.
My name is written on his hands,
my name is hidden in his heart;
I know that while in heaven he stands
no power can force me to depart (Repeat)

When Satan tempts me to despair
and tells me of the guilt within,
upward I look, and see him there
who made an end of all my sin.
Because the sinless Saviour died,
my sinful soul is counted free;
for God, the just, is satisfied
to look on him and pardon me (Repeat)

Behold him there! The risen Lamb,
my perfect, sinless righteousness,
the great unchangeable I AM,
the King of glory and of grace!
One with my Lord, I cannot die:
my soul is purchased by his blood,
my life is safe with Christ on high,
with Christ, my Saviour and my God (Repeat)

Words: Charitie L de Chenez (1841-92)

38a Alive with Christ
Colossians 2:13-15

When you were dead in your sins and in
the uncircumcision of your sinful nature,
God made you alive with Christ. He
forgave us all our sins, having cancelled the
written code, with its regulations, that was
against us and that stood opposed to us;
he took it away, nailing it to the cross.
And having disarmed the powers and
authorities, he made a public spectacle of
them, triumphing over them by the cross.

39
BEHOLD THE LORD

upon his throne; his face is shining like the sun.
With eyes blazing fire, and feet glowing bronze,
his voice like mighty waters roars.
Holy, holy, Lord God Almighty.
Holy, holy, we stand in awe of you.

The first, the last, the living One
laid down his life for all the world;
behold he now lives forever more,
and holds the keys of death and hell.
Holy, holy, Lord God Almighty;
Holy, holy, we bow before your throne.

So let our praises ever ring
to Jesus Christ, our glorious King.
All heaven and earth resound as we cry:
'Worthy is the Son of God!'
Holy, holy, Lord God Almighty;
Holy, holy, we fall down at your feet.

Noel Richards & Gerald Coates
Copyright © 1991 Kingsway's Thankyou Music.

40
BIND US TOGETHER

Lord, bind us together
with cords that cannot be broken.
Bind us together, Lord, bind us together,
bind us together with love.

There is only one God, there is only one King;
there is only one body, that is why we sing:

Made for the glory of God,
purchased by his precious Son;
born with the right to be clean,
for Jesus the victory has won.

You are the family of God,
you are the promise divine;
you are God's chosen desire,
you are the glorious new wine.

Bob Gillman
Copyright © 1977 Kingsway's Thankyou Music.

41
BLESSED BE THE NAME OF THE LORD

(Repeat x3)
For he is our Rock,
for he is our Rock, he is the Lord (Repeat)

Jesus reigns on high in all the earth (Repeat x3)
The universe is in the hands of the Lord (Repeat)

Kevin Prosch & Danny Daniels
Copyright © 1989 Mercy/Vineyard Publishing/Adm. by CopyCare

41a A creed

Leader We proclaim the church's faith
in Jesus Christ.

**All We believe and declare that our
Lord Jesus Christ, the Son of God,
is both divine and human.**

Leader God, of the being of the Father,
the only Son from before time began;
human from the being of his mother
born in the world;

**All fully God and fully human;
human in both mind and body.**

Leader As God he is equal to the Father,
as human he is less than the Father.

**All Although he is both
divine and human
he is not two beings but one Christ.**

Leader One, not by turning God into flesh,
but by taking humanity into God;

**All truly one, not by mixing humanity
with Godhead,
but by being one person.**

Leader For as mind and body form one
human being so the one Christ is
both divine and human.

**All The Word became flesh and lived
among us; we have seen his glory,
the glory of the only Son from the
Father, full of grace and truth.**

*From the Athanasian Creed. From Common Worship:
Services and Prayers for the Church of England.*

42
BLESSING AND HONOUR
glory and power be unto the Ancient of Days;
from every nation, all of creation
bow before the Ancient of Days.

*Every tongue in heaven and earth
shall declare your glory,
every knee shall bow at your throne in worship;
you will be exalted, O God,
and your kingdom shall not pass away,
O Ancient of Days.*

Your kingdom shall reign over all the earth:
sing unto the Ancient of Days.
For none shall compare to your matchless worth:
sing unto the Ancient of Days.

*Jamie Harvill & Gary Sadler. Copyright © 1992
Integrity's Praise! Music/Adm. by Kingsway's Thankyou Music*

43
BLESS THE LORD, O MY SOUL
*bless the Lord, O my soul,
and all that is within me
bless his holy name.
(Repeat)*

King of kings (for ever and ever)
Lord of lords (for ever and ever)
King of kings (for ever and ever)
King of kings and Lord of lords.

Bless the Lord...

Author unknown

44
BREATHE ON ME, BREATH OF GOD
fill me with life anew,
that as you love, so I may love
and do what you would do.

Breathe on me, breath of God,
until my heart is pure,
until my will is one with yours
to do and to endure.

Breathe on me, breath of God;
fulfil my heart's desire,
until this earthly part of me
glows with your heavenly fire.

Breathe on me, breath of God;
so shall I never die,
but live with you the perfect life
of your eternity.

*Edwin Hatch (1835-89)
in this version Jubilate Hymns*

45
BREATHE ON ME, BREATH OF GOD
and fill my life anew;
that I may love as you love,
and do the works that you do.
Holy Spirit, breathe on me.

Breathe on me, breath of God,
until my heart is pure;
until my will is one with yours
let holiness and love endure.
Holy Spirit, breathe on me.

*And let every part of me glow with fire divine;
with passion in my life, Jesus, let your glory shine.
(Repeat)*

*Edwin Hatch (1835-89) & David Fellingham
Words adaption copyright © 1995 Kingsway's Thankyou Music*

45a The fruit of the Spirit
Galatians 5:22-23

The fruit of the Spirit is love, joy,
peace, patience, kindness, goodness,
faithfulness, gentleness and self-control.
Against such things there is no law.

46
BREATHE ON ME, SPIRIT OF JESUS.
Breathe on me, Holy Spirit of God.

Fill me again, Spirit of Jesus.
Fill me again, Holy Spirit of God.

Change my heart, Spirit of Jesus.
Change my heart, Holy Spirit of God.

Bring peace to the world, Spirit of Jesus.
Bring peace to the world, Holy Spirit of God.

Tina Pownall
Copyright © 1987 Sovereign Music UK

47
BROKEN FOR ME
broken for you,
the body of Jesus, broken for you.

He offered his body, he poured out his soul;
Jesus was broken, that we might be whole:

Come to my table and with me dine;
eat of my bread and drink of my wine.

This is my body given for you;
eat it remembering I died for you.

This is my blood I shed for you;
for your forgiveness, making you new.

Janet Lunt
Copyright © 1978 Sovereign Music UK

48
BROTHER, LET ME BE YOUR SERVANT
let me be as Christ to you;
pray that I may have the grace
to let you be my servant, too.

We are pilgrims on a journey,
we are brothers on the road;
we are here to help each other
walk the mile and bear the load.

I will hold the Christ light for you
in the night-time of your fear;
I will hold my hand out to you,
speak the peace you long to hear.

I will weep when you are weeping,
when you laugh I'll laugh with you;
I will share your joy and sorrow
'till we've seen this journey through.

When we sing to God in heaven
we shall find such harmony,
born of all we've known together
of Christ's love and agony.

Brother, let me be your servant,
let me be as Christ to you;
pray that I may have the grace
to let you be my servant, too.

Richard Gillard. Copyright © 1977 Scripture in Song,
a division of Integrity Music/Adm. by Kingsway's Thankyou Music

49
BY HIS GRACE
we are redeemed, by his blood we are made clean,
and we now can know him face to face.
By his pow'r we have been raised,
hidden now in Christ by faith,
we will praise the glory of his grace.

Steven Fry. Copyright © 1994 Deep Fryed Music
/Word Music Inc/Maranatha! Music admin by CopyCare

50
BY YOUR SIDE
I would stay; in your arms I would lay.
Jesus, lover of my soul,
nothing from you I withhold.

Lord, I love you, and adore you;
what more can I say?
You cause my love to grow stronger
with every passing day.
(Repeat)

Noel & Tricia Richards
Copyright © 1989 Kingsway's Thankyou Music

51
CAN A NATION BE CHANGED?
Can a nation be saved?
Can a nation be turned back to you?
(Repeat)

We're on our knees, we're on our knees again.
We're on our knees, we're on our knees again.

Let this nation be changed,
let this nation be saved,
let this nation be turned back to you.
(Repeat)

Matt Redman
Copyright © 1996 Kingsway's Thankyou Music.

52
CALLED TO A BATTLE, HEAVENLY WAR;
though we may struggle, victory is sure.
Death will not triumph, though we may die;
Jesus has promised our eternal life.

By the blood of the Lamb we shall overcome,
see the accuser thrown down.
By the word of the Lord we shall overcome,
raise a victory cry, like thunder in the skies,
thunder in the skies.

Standing together, moving as one;
we are God's army, called to overcome.
We are commissioned, Jesus says go;
in every nation, let his love be known.

Noel & Tricia Richards
Copyright © 1992 Kingsway's Thankyou Music

53
CAN I ASCEND
the hill of the Lord?
Can I stand in that holy place?
There to approach the glory of my God;
come towards to seek your face.
Purify my heart, and purify my hands,
for I know it is on holy ground I'll stand.

I'm coming up the mountain, Lord;
I'm seeking you and you alone.
I know that I will be transformed,
my heart unveiled before you.
I'm longing for your presence, Lord;
envelop me within the cloud.
I'm coming up the mountain, Lord,
my heart unveiled before you,
I will come.

I'm coming to worship,
I'm coming to bow down,
I'm coming to meet with you.
(Repeat)

Matt Redman
Copyright © 1995 Kingsway's Thankyou Music

54
CELEBRATE JESUS, CELEBRATE!
(Repeat x3)

He is risen, he is risen,
and he lives forever more.
He is risen, he is risen,
come on and celebrate
the resurrection of our Lord.

Gary Oliver. Copyright © 1988 Integrity's Hosanna! Music
Adm. Kingsway's Thankyou Music

55
CHANGE MY HEART, O GOD
make it ever true;
change my heart,
O God, may I be like you.

You are the potter, I am the clay;
mould me and make me, this is what I pray.

Eddie Espinosa. Copyright © 1982
Mercy/Vineyard Publishing admin by CopyCare

56
CHRIST IS RISEN!
Hallelujah, hallelujah!
Christ is risen! Risen indeed, hallelujah!

Love's work is done, the battle is won:
where now, O death, is your sting?
He rose again to rule and to reign,
Jesus our conquering King.

Lord over sin, Lord over death,
at his feet Satan must fall!
Every knee bow, all will confess
Jesus is Lord over all!

Tell it abroad 'Jesus is Lord!'
Shout it and let your praise ring!
Gladly we raise our songs of praise,
worship is our offering.

Chris Rolinson
Copyright © 1989 Kingsway's Thankyou Music.

57
CHRIST TRIUMPHANT, EVER REIGNING
Saviour, Master, King,
Lord of heaven, our lives sustaining,
hear us as we sing:

Yours the glory and the crown,
the high renown, the eternal name.

Word incarnate, truth revealing,
Son of Man on earth!
Power and majesty concealing
by your humble birth:

Suffering servant, scorned, ill-treated,
victim crucified!
Death is through the cross defeated,
sinners justified:

Priestly King, enthroned forever
high in heaven above!
Sin and death and hell shall never
stifle hymns of love:

So, our hearts and voices raising
through the ages long,
ceaselessly upon you gazing,
this shall be our song:

58
CHRIST'S IS THE WORLD
in which we move,
Christ's are the folk we're summoned to love,
Christ's is the voice which calls us to care,
and Christ is the One who meets us here.

To the lost Christ shows his face;
to the unloved he gives his embrace:
to those who cry in pain or disgrace,
Christ makes, with his friends, a touching place.

Feel for the people we most avoid –
strange or bereaved or never employed;
feel for the women, and feel for the men
who fear that their living is all in vain.

Feel for the parents who've lost their child,
feel for the women whom men have defiled,
feel for the baby for whom there's no breast,
and feel for the weary who find no rest.

Feel for the lives by life confused,
riddled with doubt, in loving abused;
feel for the lonely heart, conscious of sin,
which longs to be pure but fears to begin.

59
COLOURS OF DAY DAWN INTO THE MIND
the sun has come up, the night is behind.
Go down in the city, into the street,
and let's give the message to the people we meet.

So light up the fire and let the flame burn,
open the door, let Jesus return.
Take seeds of his Spirit, let the fruit grow,
tell the people of Jesus, let his love show.

Go through the park, on into the town;
the sun still shines on, it never goes down.
The light of the world is risen again;
the people of darkness are needing a friend.

Open your eyes, look into the sky,
the darkness has come, the sun came to die.
The evening draws on, the sun disappears,
but Jesus is living, his Spirit is near.

60
COME AND SEE
come and see, come and see the King of love;
see the purple robe
and crown of thorns he wears.
Soldiers mock, rulers sneer,
as he lifts the cruel cross;
lone and friendless now
he climbs towards the hill.

We worship at your feet,
where wrath and mercy meet,
and a guilty world is washed by love's pure stream.
For us he was made sin, oh help me take it in.
Deep wounds of love cry out, 'Father, forgive.'
I worship, I worship, the Lamb who was slain.

Come and weep, come and mourn
for your sin that pierced him there;
so much deeper than the wounds of thorn and nail.
All our pride, all our greed,
all our fallenness and shame;
and the Lord has laid
the punishment on him.

Man of heaven, born to earth
to restore us to your heaven,
here we bow in awe beneath your searching eyes.
From your tears comes our joy,
from your death our life shall spring;
by your resurrection power we shall rise.

61
COME LET US SING
for joy to the Lord,
come let us sing for joy to the Lord,
come let us sing for joy to the Lord,
come let us sing for joy to the Lord!

Come let us sing for joy to the Lord,
let us shout aloud to the Rock of our salvation!
Come let us sing for joy to the Lord,
let us shout aloud to the Rock of our salvation!

Let us come before him with thanksgiving,
and extol him with music and song;
for the Lord, our Lord, is a great God,
the great King above all gods.

Let us bow before him in our worship,
let us kneel before God, our great King;
for he is our God, and we are his people,
that's why we shout and sing!

62

COME, LET US WORSHIP JESUS
King of nations, Lord of all.
Magnificent and glorious, just and merciful.

Jesus, King of the nations,
Jesus, Lord of all.
Jesus, King of the nations,
Lord of all.

Lavish our hearts' affection,
deepest love and highest praise.
Voice, race and language blending,
all the world amazed.

Bring tributes from the nations,
come in joyful cavalcades,
one thunderous acclamation,
one banner raised.

Come, Lord, and fill your temple,
glorify your dwelling place,
'till nations see your splendour
and seek your face.

Fear God and give him glory,
for his hour of judgement comes.
Creator, Lord Almighty, worship him alone.

Graham Kendrick
Copyright © 1992 Make Way Music

63

COME AND PRAISE HIM
royal priesthood,
come and worship, holy nation.
Worship Jesus, our Redeemer,
he is precious, King of glory.

Andy Carter
Copyright © 1977 Kingsway's Thankyou Music

64

COME, NOW IS THE TIME TO WORSHIP
Come, now is the time to give your heart.
Come, just as you are to worship.
Come, just as you are before your God.
Come.

One day every tongue will confess you are God.
One day every knee will bow.
Still, the greatest treasure remains
for those who gladly choose you now.

Come , now is the time...

... Come, come, come.

Brian Doerksen. Copyright © 1998
Vineyard Songs (UK/Eire), admin by CopyCare

65

COME ON AND CELEBRATE
his gift of love, we will celebrate
the Son of God who loved us and gave us life.
We'll shout your praise, O King,
you give us joy nothing else can bring,
we'll give to you our offering
in celebration praise.

Come on and celebrate, celebrate,
celebrate and sing,
celebrate and sing to the King.
Come on and celebrate, celebrate,
celebrate and sing,
celebrate and sing to the King.

Trish Morgan & Dave Bankhead
Copyright © 1984 Kingsway's Thankyou Music

66

CROWN HIM WITH MANY CROWNS
the Lamb upon his throne;
hark, how the heavenly anthem drowns
all music but its own!
Awake, my soul, and sing
of him who died for thee,
and hail him as thy matchless King
through all eternity.

Crown him the Lord of life,
who triumphed o'er the grave
and rose victorious in the strife
for those he came to save:
his glories now we sing,
who died and rose on high,
who died eternal life to bring
and lives that death may die.

Crown him the Lord of love;
behold his hands and side,
those wounds yet visible above
in beauty glorified:
no angel in the sky
can fully bear that sight,
but downward bends his burning eye
at mysteries so bright.

Crown him the Lord of peace,
whose power a sceptre sways
From pole to pole, that wars may cease,
and all be prayer and praise:
his reign shall know no end,
and round his piercèd feet
fair flowers of paradise extend
their fragrance ever sweet.

Crown him the Lord of years,
the Potentate of time,
Creator of the rolling spheres,
ineffably sublime!
All hail, Redeemer, hail!
For thou hast died for me;
thy praise shall never, never fail
throughout eternity.

Matthew Bridges (1800-94)
& Godfrey Thring (1823-1903)

67
CREATE IN ME

a clean heart, O God,
and renew a right spirit in me.
Create in me a clean heart, O God,
and renew a right spirit in me.

Wash me, cleanse me, purify me,
make my heart as white as snow.
Create in me a clean heart, O God,
and renew a right spirit in me.

David Fellingham
Copyright © 1983 Kingsway's Thankyou Music

68
DAYS OF HEAVEN

here on the earth:
touched by power, touched by love.
By your word, and by your Spirit
you send your blessing here on us.

Lord, send the rain,
let your Spirit come and glorify Jesus.
Lord, send the rain,
let your Spirit come like a pent up flood,
driven by the breath of God.

We bring our worship, we see your face;
we stand in wonder of your grace.
Your kingdom presence, your majesty;
Jesus, you're here now, hear our plea.

David Fellingham
Copyright © 1994 Kingsway's Thankyou Music

69
DARKNESS LIKE A SHROUD

covers the earth; evil like a cloud covers the people.
But the Lord will rise upon you,
and his glory will appear on you –
nations will come to your light.

Arise, shine, your light has come,
the glory of the Lord has risen on you!
Arise, shine, your light has come,
Jesus the Light of the world has come.

Children of the light, be clean and pure.
Rise, you sleepers, Christ will shine on you.
Take the Spirit's flashing two-edged sword
and with faith declare God's mighty word;
stand up and in his strength be strong.

Here among us now, Christ the light
kindles brighter flames in our trembling hearts.
Living Word, our lamp, come guide our feet
as we walk as one in light and peace,
till justice and truth shine like the sun.

Like a city bright so let us blaze;
lights in every street turning night to day.
And the darkness shall not overcome
till the fulness of Christ's kingdom comes,
dawning to God's eternal day.

Graham Kendrick
Copyright © 1985 Kingsway's Thankyou Music

70
DID YOU FEEL
THE MOUNTAINS TREMBLE?

Did you hear the oceans roar,
when the people rose to sing of
Jesus Christ, the risen One?

Did you feel the people tremble?
Did you hear the singers roar,
when the lost began to sing of
Jesus Christ, the saving One?

And we can see that God, you're moving,
a mighty river through the nations.
And young and old will turn to Jesus.
Fling wide you heavenly gates,
prepare the way of the risen Lord.

Open up the doors and let the music play,
let the streets resound with singing.
Songs that bring your hope,
songs that bring your joy,
dancers who dance upon injustice.

Do you feel the darkness tremble,
when all the saints join in one song,
and all the streams flow as one river,
to wash away our brokenness?

And we can see that God, you're moving,
a time of jubilee is coming,
when young and old will turn to Jesus.
Fling wide you heavenly gates,
prepare the way of the risen Lord.

Open up the doors...

Martin Smith. Copyright © 1994 Curious? Music UK
Adm by Kingsway's Thankyou Music

17

71

DO NOT BE AFRAID

for I have redeemed you.
I have called you by your name;
you are mine.

When you walk through the waters I'll be with you;
you will never sink beneath the waves.

When the fire is burning all around you,
you will never be consumed by the flames.

When the fear of loneliness is looming,
then remember I am at your side.

When you dwell in the exile of the stranger,
remember you are precious in my eyes.

You are mine, O my child, I am your Father,
and I love you with a perfect love.

Gerald Markland
Copyright © Kevin Mayhew Ltd

72

DON'T LET MY LOVE GROW COLD

I'm calling out, 'light the fire again.'
Don't let my vision die;
I'm calling out, 'light the fire again.'

You know my heart, my deeds;
I'm calling out, 'light the fire again.'
I need your discipline;
I'm calling out, 'light the fire again.'

I am here to buy gold, refined in the fire:
naked and poor, wretched and blind, I come.
Clothe me in white, so I won't be ashamed:
Lord, light the fire again!

Brian Doerksen . Copyright © 1994
Mercy/Vineyard Publishing/adm. by CopyCare

73

DOWN THE MOUNTAIN

the river flows
and it brings refreshing wherever it goes.
Through the valleys and over the fields,
The river is rushing and the river is here.

The river of God sets our feet a-dancing,
the river of God fills our heart with cheer;
the river of God fills our mouths with laughter,
and we rejoice for the river is here.

The river God is teeming with life,
and all who touch it can be revived.
And those who linger on this river's shore
will come back thirsting for more of the Lord.

Up to the mountain we love to go
to find the presence of the Lord.
Along the banks of the river we run,
we dance with laughter, giving praise to the Son.

Andy Park. Copyright © 1994
Mercy/Vineyard Publishing/adm. by CopyCare

74

DRAW ME CLOSER, LORD

Draw me closer, dear Lord,
so that I might touch you,
so that I might touch you,
Lord, I want to touch you.

Touch my eyes, Lord,
touch my eyes, dear Lord,
so that I might see you,
so that I might see you,
Lord, I want to see you.

Your glory and your love (x3)
and your majesty.

Stuart DeVane & Glenn Gore. Copyright © 1987
Mercy/Vineyard Publishing/admin by CopyCare

75

DRAW ME CLOSE TO YOU,

never let me go.
I lay it all down again,
to hear you say that I'm your friend.

You are my desire, no one else will do,
'cause nothing else could take your place,
to feel the warmth of your embrace.
Help me find the way,
bring me back to you.

You're all I want, you're all I've ever needed.
You're all I want, help me know you are near.

(Last time chorus)
You're all I want, you're all I've ever needed.
You're all I want, help me know you are here.

Kelly Carpenter. Copyright © 1994
Mercy/Vineyard Publishing admin by CopyCare

75a All I want
Psalm 27:4

One thing I ask of the Lord, this is
what I seek; that I may dwell in the
house of the Lord all the days of my life,
to gaze upon the beauty of the Lord
and to seek him in his temple.

76
EMMANUEL, EMMANUEL
we call your name, Emmanuel.
God with us, revealed in us,
we call your name, Emmanuel.

Bob McGee
Copyright © 1976 C.A. Music admin by CopyCare

77
EL-SHADDAI
El-Shaddai,
El-Elyon na Adonai,
age to age you're still the same
by the power of the name.
El-Shaddai, El-Shdddai,
Erkamka na Adonai,
we will praise and lift you high.
El-Shaddai.

Through your love and through the ram
you saved the son of Abraham;
through the power of your hand,
turned the sea into dry land.
To the outcast on her knees
you were the God who really sees,
and by your might you set your children free.

Through the years you made it clear
that the time of Christ was near,
though the people couldn't see
what Messiah ought to be.
Though your word contained the plan,
they just could not understand
your most awesome work was done
through the frailty of your Son.

Michael Card & John Thompson. Copyright © 1981
Whole Armor & Full Armor Publishing admin by TKO Publishing Ltd

78
EXALT THE LORD OUR GOD
exalt the Lord our God,
and worship at his footstool,
worship at his footstool;
holy is he, holy is he.

Rick Ridings. Copyright © 1977, 1980 Scripture in Song,
a division of Integrity Music/Adm. by Kingsway's Thankyou Music.

79
FAITHFUL GOD, FAITHFUL GOD
all sufficient One, I worship you.
Shalom my peace, my strong deliverer,
I lift you up, faithful God.

Chris Bowater
Copyright © 1990 Sovereign Lifestyle Music

80
FAITHFUL ONE, SO UNCHANGING
ageless one, you're my rock of peace.
Lord of all, I depend on you,
I call out to you again and again.
I call out to you again and again.
You are my rock in times of trouble,
you lift me up when I fall down;
all through the storm your love is the anchor,
my hope is in you alone.

Brian Doerksen
Copyright © 1989 Mercy/Vineyard Publishing/Adm. by CopyCare

81
FAR ABOVE ALL OTHER LOVES
far beyond all other joys,
heaven's blessings poured on me,
by the Holy Spirit's power.

Love's compelling power draws my heart into yours;
Jesus, how I love you, you're my friend and my Lord.
You have died and risen so what else can I say?
How I love you Lord, love you, Lord.

All ambition now has gone,
pleasing you my only goal;
motivated by your grace, living for eternity.

Looking with the eye of faith
for the day of your return;
in that day I want to stand
unashamed before your throne.

David Fellingham
Copyright © 1997 Kingsway's Thankyou Music

82
FAR AND NEAR
hear the call, worship him, Lord of all;
families of nations come,
celebrate what God has done.

Deep and wide is the love heaven sent from above;
God's own Son for sinners died,
rose again, he is alive.

Say it loud, say it strong,
tell the world what God has done;
say it loud, praise his name,
let the earth rejoice for the Lord reigns.

At his name let praise begin,
oceans roar, nature sing.
For he comes to judge the earth
in righteousness and in his truth.

Graham Kendrick
Copyright © 1996 Make Way Music

83
FATHER GOD, FILL THIS PLACE
with your love, with your grace.
As we call on your name, visit us in power again.

Lord, we worship you.
Lord, we worship you (Repeat)

Spirit come with your peace;
heal our wounds, bring release.
Lord we long for your touch,
fill our hearts with your love.

Dave Bilbrough
Copyright © 1995 Kingsway's Thankyou Music

84
FATHER GOD, I WONDER
how I managed to exist
without the knowledge of your parenthood
and your loving care.
But now I am your son,
I am adopted in your family,
and I can never be alone,
'cause Father God, you're there beside me.

I will sing your praises, I will sing your praises,
I will sing your praises forever more.
(Repeat)

Ian Smale
Copyright © 1984 Kingsway's Thankyou Music

85
FATHER, HEAR OUR PRAYER
that our lives may be consecrated only unto you;
cleanse us with your fire, fill us with your power
that the world may glorify your name.

Lord, have mercy on us. Christ, have mercy on us.
Lord, have mercy on us.

Andy Piercy
Copyright © 1995 IQ Music Ltd

86
FATHER I PLACE INTO YOUR HANDS
the things I cannot do.
Father, I place into your hands
the things that I've been through.
Father, I place into your hands
the way that I should go,
for I know I always can trust you.

Father, I place into your hands
my friends and family.
Father, I place into your hands
the things that trouble me.

Father, I place into your hands
the person I would be,
for I know I always can trust you.

Father, we love to see your face,
we love to hear your voice.
Father, we love to sing your praise
and in your name rejoice.
Father, we love to walk with you
and in your presence rest,
for we know we always can trust you.

Father, I want to be with you
and do the things you do.
Father, I want to speak the words
that you are speaking too.
Father, I want to love the ones
that you will draw to you,
for I know that I am one with you.

Jenny Hewer
Copyright © 1975 Kingsway's Thankyou Music

87
FATHER IN HEAVEN, HOW WE LOVE YOU
we lift your name in all the earth.
May your kingdom be established in our praises
as your people declare your mighty works.

Blessèd be the Lord God Almighty,
who was and is and is to come;
blessèd be the Lord God Almighty,
who reigns forever more.

Bob Fitts. Copyright © 1985 Scripture in Song,
a division of Integrity Music/Adm. by Kingsway's Thankyou Music

88
FATHER OF CREATION
unfold your sovereign plan.
Raise up a chosen generation
that will march through the land.
All of creation is longing
for your unveiling of power.
Would you release your anointing;
O God, let this be the hour.

Let your glory fall in this room,
let it go forth from here to the nations.
Let your fragrance rest in this place,
as we gather to seek your face.

Ruler of the nations, the world has yet to see
the full release of your promise,
the church in victory.
Turn to us, Lord, and touch us,
make us strong in your might.
Overcome our weakness,
that we could stand up and fight.

Let your glory fall...

(Men)	Let your kingdom come.
(Women)	Let your kingdom come.
(Men)	Let your will be done.
(Women)	Let your will be done.
(Men)	Let us see on earth
(Women)	Let us see on earth
(All)	the glory of your Son.

David Ruis. Copyright © 1992
Mercy/Vineyard Publishing/Adm. by CopyCare

89
FATHER OF LIFE, DRAW ME CLOSER

Lord, my heart is set on you:
let me run the race of time
with your life enfolding mine,
and let the peace of God, let it reign.

O Holy Spirit, Lord, my comfort
strengthen me, hold my head up high:
and I stand upon your truth,
bringing glory unto you,
and let the peace of God, let it reign.

O Lord, I hunger for more of you;
rise up within me, let me know your truth.
O Holy Spirit, saturate my soul,
and let the life of God fill me now,
let your healing pow'r
breathe life and make me whole,
and let the peace of God, let it reign.

Darlene Zschech. Copyright © 1995
Darlene Zschech/Hillsong Publishing/Kingsway's Thankyou Music

90
FATHER, WE ADORE YOU

Lay our lives before you, how we love you.

Jesus, we adore you...

Spirit, we adore you...

Terrye Coelho. Copyright © 1972
Maranatha! Music/admin by CopyCare

91
FATHER, WE LOVE YOU

we worship and adore you,
glorify your name in all the earth.
Glorify your name, glorify your name,
glorify your name in all the earth.

Jesus, we love you...

Spirit, we love you...

Donna Adkins. Copyright © 1976, 1981
Maranatha! Music/admin by CopyCare

92
FILLED WITH COMPASSION

for all creation,
Jesus came into a world that was lost.
There was but one way that he could save us,
only through suffering death on a cross.

God, you are waiting, your heart is breaking
for all the people who live on the earth.
Stir us to action, filled with your passion
for all the people who live on the earth.

Great is your passion for all the people
living and dying without knowing you.
Having no Saviour, they're lost forever,
if we don't speak out and lead them to you.

From every nation we shall be gathered,
millions redeemed shall be Jesus' reward.
Then he will turn and say to his Father:
'truly my suffering was worth it all.'

Noel & Tricia Richards
Copyright © 1994 Kingsway's Thankyou Music

93
FIRE! THERE'S A FIRE!
Sweet fire burning in my heart.
(Repeat)

And I will run with all of the passion
you've put in me.
I will spread the seed of the gospel everywhere.
And I can feel the power of your hand upon me.
Now I know I'll never be the same again.

For as long as you will give me breath,
my heart is so resolved,
oh, to lay my life before you, Lord,
let everything I do be to your praise.

Let me feel your tongues of fire resting upon me,
let me hear the sound of your mighty rushing wind.
Let my life be like an offering of worship,
let me be a living sacrifice of praise.

Paul Oakley
Copyright © 1995 Kingsway's Thankyou Music

94
FOCUS MY EYES

on you, O Lord, focus my eyes on you;
to worship in spirit and in truth,
focus my eyes on you.

Turn round my life to you, O Lord,
turn round my life to you;
to know from this night you've made me new,
turn round my life to you.

continued over...

Fill up my heart with praise, O Lord,
fill up my heart with praise;
to speak of your love in every place,
fill up my heart with praise.

Ian White. Copyright © 1988
Little Misty Music/Kingsway's Thankyou Music

95
FOR I'M BUILDING A PEOPLE OF POWER
and I'm making a people of praise
that will move through this land by my Spirit,
and will glorify my precious name.

Build your church, Lord,
make us strong, Lord,
join our hearts, Lord, through your Son.
Make us one, Lord,
in your body,
in the kingdom of your Son.

Dave Richards
Copyright © 1977 Kingsway's Thankyou Music

96
FOR THE JOYS AND FOR THE SORROWS
the best and worst of times,
for this moment, for tomorrow,
for all that lies behind;
fears that crowd around me,
for the failure of my plans,
for the dreams of all I hope to be,
the truth of what I am:

For this I have Jesus,
for this I have Jesus,
for this I have Jesus, I have Jesus.
(Repeat)

For the tears that flow in secret,
in the broken times,
for the moments of elation,
or the troubled mind;
for all the disappointments,
or the sting of old regrets,
all my prayers and longings
that seem unanswered yet:

For the weakness of my body,
the burdens of each day,
for the nights of doubt and worry,
when sleep has fled away;
needing reassurance,
and the will to start again,
a steely-eyed endurance,
the strength to fight and win:

Graham Kendrick
Copyright © 1994 Make Way Music

97
FOR THIS PURPOSE
Christ was revealed,
to destroy all the works
of the evil one.
Christ in us has overcome,
so with gladness we sing
and welcome his kingdom in.

(Men)   *Over sin he has conquered,*
(Women) hallelujah, he has conquered.
(Men)   *Over death victorious,*
(Women) hallelujah, victorious.
(Men)   *Over sickness he has triumphed,*
(Women) hallelujah, he has triumphed.
(All)   *Jesus reigns over all!*

In the name of Jesus we stand,
by the power of his blood
we now claim this ground.
Satan has no authority here;
powers of darkness must flee,
for Christ has the victory.

Graham Kendrick
Copyright © 1985 Kingsway's Thankyou Music

98
FOR THOU, O LORD, ART HIGH
above all the earth,
thou art exalted far above all gods.
For thou, O Lord, art high above all the earth,
thou art exalted far above all gods.

I exalt thee, I exalt thee,
I exalt thee, O Lord.
I exalt thee, I exalt thee,
I exalt thee, O Lord.

Pete Sanchez Jnr. Copyright © 1977
Pete Sanchez Jnr/ASCAP/Admin by Gabriel Music Inc

99
FOR WE SEE JESUS
enthroned on high,
clothed in his righteousness, we worship him.
Glory and honour we give unto you,
we see you in your holiness
and bow before your throne;
you are the Lord,
your name endures forever,
Jesus the name high over all.

Sue Hutchinson. Copyright © 1979
Word's Spirit of Praise Music admin by CopyCare

100

FROM HEAVEN YOU CAME

helpless babe, entered our world, your glory veiled;
not to be served but to serve,
and give your life that we might live.

This is our God, the servant King,
he calls us now to follow him,
to bring our lives as a daily offering
of worship to the servant King.

There in the garden of tears,
my heavy load he chose to bear;
his heart with sorrow was torn,
'Yet not my will but yours,' he said.

Come see his hands and his feet,
the scars that speak of sacrifice;
hands that flung stars into space
to cruel nails surrendered.

So let us learn how to serve,
and in our lives enthrone him;
each other's needs to prefer,
for it is Christ we're serving.

Graham Kendrick
Copyright © 1983 Kingsway's Thankyou Music

101

FRIEND OF SINNERS

Lord of truth,
I am falling in love with you.
Friend of sinners, Lord of truth,
I am falling in love with you.

Jesus, I love your name,
the name by which we're saved.
Jesus, I love your name,
the name by which we're saved.

Friend of sinners, Lord of truth,
I am giving my life to you.
Friend of sinners, Lord of truth,
I am giving my life to you.

Matt Redman
Copyright © 1994 Kingsway's Thankyou Music

102

FROM THE RISING OF THE SUN

to the going down of the same,
the Lord's name is to be praised.
From the rising of the sun
to the going down of the same,
the Lord's name is to be praised.

Praise ye the Lord,
praise him all ye servants of the Lord,
praise the name of the Lord.
Blessèd be the name of the Lord
from this time forth and forever more.

Paul S Deming. Copyright © 1976
Integrity's Hosanna! Music/Adm. Kingsway's Thankyou Music

103

FROM THE SQUALOR

of a borrowed stable
by the Spirit and a virgin's faith;
to the anguish and the shame of scandal
came the Saviour of the human race!
But the skies were filled
with the praise of heaven,
shepherds listen as the angels tell
of the gift of God come down to man
at the dawning of Immanuel.

King of heaven now the friend of sinners,
humble servant in the Father's hands,
filled with power and the Holy Spirit,
filled with mercy for the broken man.
Yes, he walked my road and he felt my pain,
joys and sorrows that I know so well;
yet his righteous steps give me hope again -
I will follow my Immanuel!

Through the kisses of a friend's betrayal,
he was lifted on a cruel cross;
he was punished for a world's transgressions,
he was suffering to save the lost.
He fights for breath, he fights for me,
loosing sinners from the claims of hell;
and with a shout our souls are free -
death defeated by Immanuel!

Now he's standing in the place of honour,
crowned with glory on the highest throne,
interceding for his own belovèd
till his Father calls to bring them home!
Then the skies will part as the trumpet sounds
hope of heaven or the fear of hell;
but the bride will run to her lover's arms,
giving glory to Immanuel!

Stuart Townend
Copyright © 1999 Kingsway's Thankyou Music

104

FROM THE SUN'S RISING

unto the sun's setting,
Jesus our Lord shall be great in the earth;
and all earth's kingdoms shall be his dominion,
all of creation shall sing of his worth.

continued over...

Let every heart, every voice,
every tongue join with spirits ablaze;
one in his love, we will circle the world
with the song of his praise.
O, let all his people rejoice,
and let all the earth hear his voice!

To every tongue, tribe and nation he sends us,
to make disciples, to teach and baptise.
for all authority to him is given;
now as his witnesses we shall arise.

Come let us join with the church from all nations,
cross every border, throw wide every door;
workers with him as he gathers his harvest,
till earth's far corners our Saviour adore.

Graham Kendrick
Copyright © 1988 Make Way Music

105
FROM WHERE THE SUN RISES
even to the place it goes down
we're giving you praise, giving you praise.
From sun-kissed islands,
and even where the cold wind blows
we're giving you praise, giving you praise.

Even in the night when the sun goes down,
we're giving you praise;
passing it along as the world goes round,
we're giving you praise.

We're lifting our faces,
looking at the One we all love
we're giving you praise, giving you praise.
All colours and races
joining with the angels above
we're giving you praise, giving you praise.

Graham Kendrick
Copyright © 1996 Make Way Music

106
GIVE ME A HEART OF COMPASSION
give me a hope for the lost.
Give me a passion for those
who are broken and down.
Lord, I am ready and willing
to serve the weak and the young;
help me to put into action
the words of this song.

And enable your servants,
enable your servants
to preach good news,
to preach good news.
(Repeat)

I'll sing the songs of salvation,
boldly I'll speak out your word.
I'll let them know by my life,
I will show you are Lord.
I'll tell them all about Jesus,
I'll tell them all about you;
I'm not ashamed of the gospel
or what it can do.

We're moving forward together,
as one voice boldly proclaim
the old and the young will be strong,
and we'll lift up your name
on to the streets to the people,
every man, woman and child,
and as we go you are with us,
you've given your power.

You've enabled your servants...

Jim Bailey
Copyright © 1997 Kingsway's Thankyou Music

107
GIVE THANKS
WITH A GRATEFUL HEART
give thanks to the holy One.
Give thanks because he's given
Jesus Christ, his Son.
(Repeat)

And now let the weak say 'I am strong,'
let the poor say 'I am rich,'
because of what the Lord has done for us.
(Repeat)

Henry Smith. Copyright © 1978 Integrity's Hosanna! Music
Adm. Kingsway's Thankyou Music

108
GIVE ME OIL IN MY LAMP
keep me burning.
Give me oil in my lamp, I pray.
Give me oil in my lamp, keep my burning,
keep me burning till the break of day.

Sing hosanna, sing hosanna,
sing hosanna to the King of kings.
Sing hosanna, sing hosanna,
sing hosanna to the King.

Give me joy in my heart, keep me praising...

Give me peace in my heart, keep me resting...

Give me love in my heart, keep me serving...

A Sevison

109
GO FORTH AND TELL

O church of God, awake!
God's saving news to all the nations take:
proclaim Christ Jesus, Saviour, Lord and King,
that all the world his worthy praise may sing.

Go forth and tell! God's love embraces all;
he will in grace respond to all who call:
how shall they call if they have never heard
the gracious invitation of his word?

Go forth and tell where still the darkness lies,
in wealth or want, the sinner surely dies;
give us, O Lord, concern of heart and mind,
a love like yours, compassionate and kind.

Go forth and tell! The doors are open wide:
share God's good gifts – let no one be denied;
live out your life as Christ your Lord shall choose,
your ransomed powers for his sole glory use.

Go forth and tell! O church of God, arise!
go in the strength which Christ your Lord supplies;
go till all nations his great name adore
and serve him, Lord and King forever more.

James E. Seddon (1915-83)
Words Copyright © Mrs J Seddon/Jubilate Hymns

110
GLORY, GLORY IN THE HIGHEST

glory, to the Almighty;
glory to the Lamb of God,
and glory to the Living Word;
glory to the Lamb!

I give glory, (glory)
glory, (glory)
glory, glory to the Lamb!
I give glory, (glory)
glory, (glory)
glory, glory to the Lamb!
I give glory to the Lamb!

Danny Daniels. Copyright © 1987
Mercy/Vineyard Publishing/Adm. by CopyCare

110a   Praise our King
Revelation 5:13

Then I heard every creature in heaven and on
earth and under the earth and on the sea, and
all that is in them, singing:

'To him who sits on the throne and to the
Lamb be praise and honour and glory and
power, for ever and ever!'

111
GOD FORGAVE MY SIN

in Jesus' name,
I've been born again in Jesus' name;
and in Jesus' name I come to you
to share his love as he told me to.

He said: 'Freely, freely, you have received,
freely, freely give;
go in my name, and because you believe
others will know that I live.'

All power is given in Jesus' name,
in earth and heaven in Jesus' name;
and in Jesus' name I come to you
to share his power as he told me to.

Carol Owens. Copyright © 1972 Bud John Songs Incl
EMI Christian Music Publishing admin by CopyCare

111a   Rejoice you righteous!
Psalm 32:1-2

Blessed is he whose transgressions are
forgiven, whose sins are covered.
Blessed is the man whose sin
the Lord does not count against him
and in whose spirit is no deceit.

112
GOD IS GOOD ALL THE TIME

he put a song of praise in this heart of mine;
God is good all the time!
Through the darkest night his light will shine:
God is good,
God is good all the time.

If you're walking through the valley
and there are shadows all around,
do not fear, he will guide you,
he will keep you safe and sound
'cause he has promised to never leave you
nor forsake you,
and his word is true.

We were sinners so unworthy,
still for us he chose to die:
filled us with his Holy Spirit,
now we can stand and testify
that his love is everlasting
and his mercies they will never end.

Don Moen & Paul Overstreet. Copyright © 1995
Integrity's Hosanna! Music/admin. by Kingsway's Thankyou Music

113
GOD IS GOOD,
WE SING AND SHOUT IT
God is good, we celebrate.
God is good, no more we doubt it.
God is good, we know it's true.

And when I think of his love for me,
my heart fills with praise
and I feel like dancing.
For in his heart there is room for me,
and I run with arms open wide.

Graham Kendrick
Copyright © 1985 Kingsway's Thankyou Music

114
GOD IS OUR FATHER
for he has made us his own,
made Jesus our brother
and hand in hand we'll grow together as one.

Sing praise to the Lord with the tambourine,
sing praise to the Lord with clapping hands,
sing praise to the Lord with dancing feet,
sing praise to the Lord with our voice.

La, la, la...

Alex Simons & Freda Kimmey
Copyright © 1977 Celebration/Kingsway's Thankyou Music

115
GOD OF GLORY
we exalt your name,
you who reign in majesty.
We lift our hearts to you
and we will worship, praise and magnify
your holy name.

(Men)	In power resplendent
(Women)	in power resplendent
(Men)	you reign in glory
(Women)	you reign in glory
(Men)	eternal King
(Women)	eternal King
(All)	you reign forever.

(Men)	Your word is mighty
(Women)	your word is mighty
(Men)	releasing captives
(Women)	releasing captives
(Men)	your love is gracious
(Women)	your love is gracious
(All)	you are my God.

David Fellingham
Copyright © 1982 Kingsway's Thankyou Music

116
GOD OF GRACE
I turn my face to you, I cannot hide;
my nakedness, my shame, my guilt,
are all before your eyes.
Strivings and all anguished dreams
in rags lie at my feet,
and only grace provides the way
for me to stand complete.

And your grace clothes me in righteousness,
and your mercy covers me in love.
Your life adorns and beautifies,
I stand complete in you.

Chris Bowater
Copyright © 1990 Sovereign Lifestyle Music

116a   Heirs by his grace
Titus 3:4-7

But when the kindness and love of
God our Saviour appeared, he saved us,
not because of righteous things we had done,
but because of his mercy.

He saved us through the washing of
rebirth and renewal by the Holy Spirit,
who he poured out on us generously
through Jesus Christ our Saviour, so that,
having been justified by his grace, we might
become heirs having the hope of eternal life.

117
GOD SENT HIS SON
they called him Jesus;
he came to love, heal, and forgive;
he lived and died to buy my pardon,
an empty grave is there to prove my Saviour lives.

Because he lives I can face tomorrow;
because he lives all fear is gone;
because I know he holds the future,
and life is worth the living
just because he lives.

How sweet to hold a new-born baby,
and feel the pride and joy he gives;
but greater still the calm assurance,
this child can face uncertain days because he lives.

And then one day I'll cross the river;
I'll fight life's final war with pain;
and then as death gives way to victory,
I'll see the lights of glory and I'll know he lives.

Gloria & William J Gaither. Copyright © 1971
Gaither Music Company/WJG Inc./Kingsway's Thankyou Music

118
GOOD NEWS
good news to you we bring, alleluia!
News of great joy that angels sing, alleluia!

Tender mercy he has shown us,
joy to all the world;
for us God sends his only Son, alleluia!

Let earth's dark shadows fly away, alleluia!
In Christ has dawned an endless day, alleluia!

Now God with us on earth resides, alleluia!
and heaven's door is open wide, alleluia!

Graham Kendrick
Copyright © 1988 Make Way Music

119
GREAT IS THE DARKNESS
that covers the earth,
oppression, injustice and pain.
Nations are slipping in hopeless despair,
though many have come in your name.
Watching while sanity dies,
touched by the madness and lies.

Come, Lord Jesus, come, Lord Jesus,
pour out your Spirit we pray.
Come, Lord Jesus, come, Lord Jesus,
pour out your Spirit on us today.

May now your church rise with power and love,
this glorious gospel proclaim.
In every nation salvation will come
to those who believe in your name.
Help us bring light to this world
that we might speed your return.

Great celebrations on that final day
when out of the heavens you come.
Darkness will vanish, all sorrow will end,
and rulers will bow at your throne.
Our great commission complete,
then face to face we shall meet.

Noel Richards & Gerald Coates
Copyright © 1992 Kingsway's Thankyou Music

120
GREAT IS THE LORD
and most worthy of praise,
the city of our God, the holy place,
the joy of the whole earth.
Great is the Lord in whom we have the victory,
he aids us against the enemy,
we bow down on our knees.

And Lord, we want to lift your name on high,
and Lord, we want to thank you,
for the works you've done in our lives;
and Lord, we trust in your unfailing love,
for you alone are God eternal,
throughout earth and heaven above.

Steve McEwan
Copyright © 1985 Body Songs/Adm. by CopyCare

121
GREAT IS HE WHO'S THE KING OF KINGS
and the Lord of lords,
he is wonderful!

Alleluia, alleluia,
alleluia, he is wonderful!

Alleluia, salvation and glory,
honour and power, he is wonderful!

Author unknown

122
GREAT IS YOUR FAITHFULNESS
O God my Father,
you have fulfilled all your promise to me;
you never fail and your love is unchanging –
all you have been, you forever will be.

Great is your faithfulness!
Great is your faithfulness!
Morning by morning new mercies I see;
all I have needed your hand has provided,
great is your faithfulness, Father, to me!

Summer and winter, and springtime and harvest,
sun, moon and stars in their courses above
join with all nature in eloquent witness
to your great faithfulness, mercy and love.

Pardon for sin and a peace everlasting –
your living presence to cheer and to guide;
strength for today and bright hope for tomorrow,
these are the blessings your love will provide.

Thomas Chisholm (1866-1960). Grateful thanks given
to Jubilate Hymns for the modernisation of the words.

123
GUIDE ME, O THOU GREAT JEHOVAH
pilgrim through this barren land;
I am weak, but thou art mighty,
hold me with thy powerful hand:
Bread of heaven, Bread of heaven,
feed me now and ever more,
feed me now and ever more.

continued over...

27

Open thou the crystal fountain
whence the healing stream doth flow;
let the fiery, cloudy pillar
lead me all my journey through:
strong Deliverer, strong Deliverer,
be thou still my strength and shield,
be thou still my strength and shield.

When I tread the verge of Jordan
bid my anxious fears subside;
death of death, and hell's destruction,
land me safe on Canaan's side:
songs of praises, songs of praises,
I will ever give to thee,
I will ever give to thee.

William Williams (1717-91)
trans. Peter Williams (1727-96)

124
HALLELUJAH, MY FATHER
for giving us your Son;
sending him into the world,
to be given up for men.
Knowing we would bruise him
and smite him from the earth.
Hallelujah, my Father, in his death is my birth;
hallelujah, my Father, in his life is my life.

Tim Cullen. Copyright © 1975
Celebration/Kingsway's Thankyou Music

125
HALLELUJAH, FOR THE LORD OUR GOD
the Almighty reigns
Hallelujah, for the Lord our God
the Almighty reigns.

Let us rejoice and be glad
and give the glory unto him.
Hallelujah, for the Lord our God
the Almighty reigns.

Dale Garratt. Copyright © 1972 Scripture in Song,
a division of Integrity Music/Adm. by Kingsway's Thankyou Music

125a   Hallelujah!
Revelation 19:6

Then I heard what sounded like a great
multitude, like the roar of rushing waters
and like loud peals of thunder, shouting:

'Hallelujah!
For our Lord God Almighty reigns.
Let us rejoice and be glad and give him glory!'

126
HAVE YOU HEARD THE GOOD NEWS?
Have you heard the good news?
We can live in hope
because of what the Lord has done.
(Repeat)

There is a way when there seems to be no way,
there is a light in the darkness:
there is a hope, an everlasting hope,
there is a God who can help us.

A hope for justice and a hope for peace,
a hope for those in desperation:
we have a future, if only we believe
he works in every situation.

Stuart Garrard. Copyright © 1995
Curious? Music UK/Adm. Kingsway's Thankyou Music

126a   Live in hope
1 Peter 1:3-4

Praise be to the God and Father of our
Lord Jesus Christ!
In his great mercy he has given us
new birth into a living hope
through the resurrection
of Jesus Christ from the dead,
and into an inheritance that can never perish,
spoil or fade kept in heaven for you...

127
HAVE YOU NOT SAID
as we pass through water, you will be with us?
And you have said as we walk through fire,
we will not be burned.
We are not afraid, for you are with us;
we will testify to the honour of your name.
We are witnesses, you have shown us
you are the one who can save.

Fill us up and send us out
in the power of your name.
(Repeat)

Bring them from the west, sons and daughters,
call them for your praise.
Gather from the east all your children,
coming home again.
Bring them from afar, all the nations,
from the north and south,
drawing all the peoples in.
Corners of the earth, come to see there's
only one Saviour and King.

Matt Redman
Copyright © 1995 Kingsway's Thankyou Music

128

HE BROUGHT ME TO HIS BANQUETING TABLE

(Women) he brought me to his banqueting table
(All) and his banner over me is love.
(Men) I am my Belovèd's and he is mine,
(Women) I am my Belovèd's and he is mine,
(All) and his banner over me is love.
Yes, his banner over me is love.

And we can feel the love of God in this place,
we believe your goodness, we receive your grace.
We delight ourselves at your table, O God,
you do all things well, just look at our lives.

Kevin Prosch. Copyright © 1991
Mercy/Vineyard Publishing/Adm. by CopyCare

128a   The Lover
Song of Songs 2:4

He has taken me to the banquet hall,
and his banner over me is love.

129

HE IS EXALTED

the King is exalted on high, I will praise him.
He is exalted, forever exalted
and I will praise his name!

He is the Lord, forever his truth shall reign.
Heaven and earth rejoice in his holy name.
He is exalted, the King is exalted on high!

Twila Paris. Copyright © 1985 Straightway Music/
EMI Christian Music Publishing/Adm. by CopyCare.

130

HE HAS RISEN, HE HAS RISEN

he has risen, Jesus is alive.

When the life flowed from his body,
seemed like Jesus' mission failed.
But his sacrifice accomplished,
victory over sin and hell.

In the grave God did not leave him,
for his body to decay;
raised to life, the great awakening,
Satan's power he overcame.

If there were no resurrection,
we ourselves could not be raised;
but the Son of God is living,
so our hope is not in vain.

When the Lord rides out of heaven,
mighty angels at his side,

they will sound the final trumpet,
from the grave we shall arise.

He has given life immortal,
we shall see him face to face;
through eternity we'll praise him,
Christ, the champion of our faith.

Gerald Coates, Noel & Tricia Richards
Copyright © 1993 Kingsway's Thankyou Music

131

HE'S GIVEN ME A GARMENT OF PRAISE

instead of a spirit of despair;
he's given me a garment of praise
instead of a spirit of despair.
(Repeat)

A crown of beauty instead of ashes,
the oil of gladness instead of mourning –
my soul rejoices as I delight myself in God.

David J Hadden. Copyright © 1994
Restoration Music admin. By Sovereign Music UK

132

HE IS LORD, HE IS LORD

he is risen from the dead and he is Lord.
Every knee shall bow,
every tongue confess
that Jesus Christ is Lord.

Author unknown

133

HE IS THE LORD

and he reigns on high: he is the Lord.
Spoke into the darkness, created the light:
he is the Lord.
Who is like unto him, never ending in days?
He is the Lord.
And he comes in power when we call on his name:
he is the Lord.

Show your power, O Lord our God (Repeat)
our God.

Your gospel, O Lord, is the hope for our nation:
you are the Lord.
It's the power of God for our salvation:
you are the Lord.
We ask not for riches, but look to the cross:
you are the Lord.
And for our inheritance give us the lost:
you are the Lord.

Send your power ...

Kevin Prosch. Copyright © 1991
Mercy/Vineyard Publishing/Adm. by CopyCare

134

HE THAT IS IN US

is greater than he
that is in the world.
He that is in us is greater than he
that is in the world.

Therefore I will sing and I will rejoice
for his Spirit lives in me.
Christ the living One has overcome
and we share in his victory.

All the powers of death and hell and sin
lie crushed beneath his feet;
Jesus owns the name above all names,
crowned with honour and majesty.

Graham Kendrick
Copyright © 1986 Kingsway's Thankyou Music

134a   A litany

Leader By the mystery of your holy
incarnation; by your birth,
childhood and obedience; by your
baptism, fasting and temptation,
All   good Lord, deliver us.

Leader By your ministry in word and work;
by your mighty acts of power; and
by your preaching of the kingdom,
All   good Lord, deliver us.

Leader By your agony and trial;
by your cross and passion; and
by your precious death and burial,
All   good Lord, deliver us.

Leader By your mighty resurrection;
by your glorious ascension; and by
your sending of the Holy Spirit,
All   good Lord, deliver us.

From Common Worship:
Services and Prayers for the Church of England.

135

HE WALKED WHERE I WALKED

(echo after each line)
he stood where I stand
he felt what I feel
he understands.
He knows my frailty,
shared my humanity,
tempted in every way,
yet without sin.

(All)   God with us, so close to us
God with us, Immanuel!
(Repeat)

One of a hated race,
stung by the prejudice,
suffering injustice,
yet he forgives.
Wept for my wasted years,
paid for my wickedness,
he died in my place
that I might live.

Graham Kendrick
Copyright © 1988 Make Way Music

136

HE WAS PIERCED

for our transgressions,
and bruised for our iniquities;
and to bring us peace he was punished,
and by his stripes we are healed.

He was led like a lamb to the slaughter,
although he was innocent of crime;
and cut off from the land of the living,
he paid for the guilt that was mine.

We like sheep have gone astray,
turned each one to his own way,
and the Lord has laid on him
the iniquity of us all.

(Descant)
Like a lamb, like a lamb
to the slaughter he came.
And the Lord laid on him the iniquity of us all.

Maggi Dawn
Copyright © 1987 Kingsway's Thankyou Music

137

HEAR THESE PRAISES

from a grateful heart,
each time I think of you the praises start:
love you so much, Jesus, love you so much.

Lord I love you, my soul sings,
in your presence, carried on your wings:
love you so much, Jesus, love you so much.

How my soul longs for you,
longs to worship you forever
in your power and majesty.
Lift my hands, lift my heart,
lift my voice towards the heavens,
for you are my sun and shield.

Russell Fragar. Copyright © 1996
Russell Fragar/Hillsong Publishing/Kingsway's Thankyou Music

137a To dwell in God's presence
Psalm 84:10-12

Better is one day in your courts
than a thousand elsewhere;
I would rather be a doorkeeper
in the house of my God
than dwell in the tents of the wicked.
For the Lord God is a sun and shield;
the Lord bestows favour and honour;
no good thing does he withhold
from those whose walk is blameless.
O Lord Almighty
    blessed is the man who trusts in you.

138
HERE I AM, AND I HAVE COME
to thank you, Lord, for all you've done;
thank you, Lord.
You paid the price at Calvary,
you shed your blood, you set me free;
thank you, Lord.
No greater love was ever shown,
no better life ever was laid down.

And I will always love your name;
and I will always sing your praise.
(Repeat)

You took my sin, you took my shame,
you drank my cup, you bore my pain;
thank you, Lord.
You broke the curse, you broke the chains,
in victory from death you rose again;
thank you, Lord.
And not by works, but by your grace
you clothe me now in your righteousness.

You bid me come, you make me whole,
you give me peace, you restore my soul;
thank you, Lord.
You fill me up, and when I'm full,
you give me more till I overflow;
thank you, Lord.
You're making me to be like you,
to do the works of the Father, too.

139
HERE I AM ONCE AGAIN
I pour out my heart for I know that you hear
every cry; you are listening,
no matter what state my heart is in.

You are faithful to answer
with words that are true and a hope that is real.
As I feel your touch,
you bring a freedom to all that's within.

In the safety of this place
I'm longing to

Pour out my heart, to say that I love you,
pour out my heart, to say that I need you.
Pour out my heart, to say that I'm thankful,
pour out my heart, to say that you're wonderful.

140
HERE I AM, WHOLLY AVAILABLE
as for me, I will serve the Lord.
Here I am, wholly available;
as for me, I will serve the Lord.

The fields are white unto harvest,
but O, the labourers are so few;
so Lord, I give myself to help the reaping,
to gather precious souls unto you.

The time is right in the nation
for works of power and authority;
God's looking for a people who are willing
to be counted in his glorious victory.

As salt are we ready to savour?
In darkness are we ready to be light?
God's seeking out a very special people
to manifest his truth and his might.

140a 'Send me'
Isaiah 6:8

Then I heard the voice of the Lord saying,
'Whom shall I send?
And who will go for us?'
And I said,
'Here am I.
Send me!'

141
HERE IS BREAD
here is wine
Christ is with us
he is with us;
break the bread, drink the wine
Christ is with us here.

continued over...

31

Here is grace, here is peace,
Christ is with us, he is with us;
know his grace, find his peace
feast on Jesus here.

In this bread there is healing,
in this cup there's life forever;
in this moment, by the Spirit
Christ is with us here.

Here we are, joined in one,
Christ is with us, he is with us;
we'll proclaim, till he comes Jesus crucified.

Graham Kendrick
Copyright © 1992 Make Way Music

142
HERE IS THE RISEN SON
riding out in glory,
radiating light all around.
Here is the Holy Spirit,
poured out for the nations,
glorifying Jesus the Lamb.

We will stand as a people
who are upright and holy,
we will worship the Lord of hosts.
We will watch, we will wait
on the walls of the city,
we will look and see what he will say to us.

Every knee shall bow before him,
every tongue confess
that he is King of kings, Lord of lords,
and ruler of the earth.

Michael Sandeman
Copyright © 1997 Kingsway's Thankyou Music

143
HERE IS LOVE VAST AS THE OCEAN
loving kindness as the flood,
when the Prince of life, our ransom
shed for us his precious blood.
Who his love will not remember?
Who can cease to sing his praise?
He can never be forgotten
throughout heaven's eternal days.

On the mount of crucifixion
fountains opened deep and wide;
through the floodgates of God's mercy
flowed a vast and gracious tide.
Grace and love, like mighty rivers,
poured incessant from above,
and heaven's peace and perfect justice
kissed a guilty world in love.

William Rees

144
HIS NAME IS WONDERFUL
his name is wonderful,
his name is wonderful,
Jesus my Lord.
He is the mighty King,
master of everything,
his name is wonderful,
Jesus my Lord.

He's the great shepherd,
the rock of all ages,
Almighty God is he.
Bow down before him,
love and adore him,
his name is wonderful,
Jesus my Lord.

Audrey Meir. Copyright © 1959,1987
Manna Music Inc/Kingsway's Thankyou Music

145
HIS LOVE
is higher than the highest of mountains.
His love goes deeper that the deepest of seas.
His love, it stretches to the farthest horizon,
and his love, it reaches to me.

His love is stronger than the angels and demons.
His love, it keeps me in my life's darkest hour.
His love secures me on the pathway to heaven,
and his love is my strength and power.

His love is sweeter than the sweetest of honey.
His love is better than the choicest of wine.
His love, it satisfies the deepest of hunger,
and his love, in Jesus it's mine.

Your love is higher...

David Ruis.. Copyright © 1992
Mercy/Vineyard Publishing/Adm. by CopyCare

145a   God's love endures
Romans 8:37-39

No, in all these things we are more than
conquerors through him who loved us.
For I am convinced that neither death nor
life, neither angels nor demons, neither the
present nor the future, nor any powers,
neither height nor depth, nor anything else in
all creation, will be able to separate us from
the love of God that is in Christ Jesus our
Lord.

146

HOLD ME LORD

(Women) Hold me Lord
(Men) in your arms
(Women) in your arms
(Men) fill me Lord,
(Women) fill me Lord,
(All) with your Spirit.

(Men) Touch my heart
(Women) Touch my heart
(Men) with your love,
(Women) with your love,
(Men) let my life
(Women) let my life
(All) glorify your name

Singing alleluia,
singing alleluia,
singing alleluia,
singing alleluia.

Alleluia (Alleluia)
Allelu (Allelu)
Alleluia (Alleluia)
Allelu (Allelu)

Danny Daniels. Copyright © 1982
Mercy/Vineyard Publishing/Adm. by CopyCare

147

HOLD ME CLOSER TO YOU EACH DAY

May my love for you never fade.
Keep my focus on all that's true;
may I never lose sight of you.

In my failure, in my success,
if in sadness or happiness,
be the hope I am clinging to,
for my heart belongs to you.

You are only a breath away,
watching over me every day;
in my heart I am filled with peace
when I hear you speak to me.

No one loves me the way you do,
no one cares for me like you do.
Feels like heaven has broken through;
God, you know how I love you.

Noel & Tricia Richards
Copyright © 1996 Kingsway's Thankyou Music

148

HOLINESS UNTO THE LORD

unto the King.
Holiness unto your name I will sing.

Holiness unto Jesus,
holiness unto you, Lord.
Holiness unto Jesus,
holiness unto you, Lord.

I love you, I love your ways,
I love your name.
I love you, and all my days I'll proclaim:

Danny Daniels. Copyright © 1989
Mercy/Vineyard Publishing admin by CopyCare

149

HOLY, HOLY, HOLY, HOLY

holy, holy, Lord God Almighty!
And we lift our hearts before you
as a token of our love:
holy, holy, holy, holy.

Gracious Father, gracious Father,
we're so glad to be your children, gracious Father;
and we lift our heads before you
as a token of our love,
gracious Father, gracious Father.

Precious Jesus, precious Jesus,
we're so glad that you've redeemed us,
precious Jesus;
and we lift our hands before you
as a token of our love,
precious Jesus, precious Jesus,

Holy Spirit, Holy Spirit,
come and fill our hearts anew, Holy Spirit;
and we lift our voice before you
as a token of our love,
Holy Spirit, Holy Spirit.

Hallelujah, hallelujah,
hallelujah, hallelujah
and we lift our hearts before you
as a token of our love,
hallelujah, hallelujah.

Jimmy Collins Owens. Copyright © 1972 Bud John Songs/
EMI Christian Music Publishing/Adm. by CopyCare

150

HOLY, HOLY, HOLY IS THE LORD

holy is the Lord God Almighty.
(Repeat)
who was and is and is to come,
holy, holy, holy is the Lord.

Worthy, worthy, worthy is the Lord...

Jesus, Jesus, Jesus is the Lord...

Glory, glory, glory to the Lord...

Author unknown

151

HOLY, HOLY, HOLY
IS THE LORD GOD ALMIGHTY

Holy, holy, holy is the Lord God Almighty
Who was and is and is to come (Repeat)

Lift up his name with the sound of singing,
lift up his name in all the earth.
Lift up your voice and give him glory,
for he is worthy to be praised.

Nathan Fellingham
Copyright © 1995 Kingsway's Thankyou Music

151a Holy is the Lord
Revelation 4:8b-11

'Holy, holy, holy is the Lord God Almighty,
who was, and is, and is to come.'
Whenever the living creatures give glory,
honour and thanks to him who sits on the
throne and who lives for ever and ever,
the twenty-four elders fall down
before him who sits on the throne,
and worship him who lives for ever and ever.
They lay their crowns before the throne
and say:
'You are worthy, our Lord and God,
to receive glory and honour and power,
for you created all things, and by your will
they were created and have their being.'

152

HOLY, HOLY, HOLY,
LORD GOD ALMIGHTY

early in the morning our song shall rise to thee:
holy, holy, holy, merciful and mighty,
God in three persons, blessèd Trinity!

Holy, holy, holy! All the saints adore thee,
casting down their golden crowns
around the glassy sea;
cherubim and seraphim falling down before thee,
who was, and is, and ever more shall be.

Holy, holy, holy! Though the darkness hide thee,
though the eye of sinful man thy glory may not see;
only thou art holy, there is none beside thee,
perfect in power, in love and purity.

Holy, holy, holy, Lord God Almighty!
All thy works shall praise thy name
in earth, and sky, and sea;
holy, holy, holy, merciful and mighty,
God in three persons, blessèd Trinity!

Reginald Heber (1783-1826)

153

HOSANNA

hosanna, hosanna in the highest.
(Repeat)
Lord we lift up your name,
with hearts full of praise,
be exalted, O Lord, my God,
hosanna in the highest.

Glory, glory, glory to the King of kings.
Glory, glory, glory to the King of kings.
Lord, we lift up your name,
with hearts full of praise,
be exalted, O Lord, my God,
glory to the King of kings.

Carl Tuttle. Copyright © 1985
Mercy/Vineyard Publishing admin by CopyCare

154

HOLY SPIRIT, WE WELCOME YOU

Holy Spirit, we welcome you.
Move among us with holy fire,
as we lay aside all earthly desires,
hands reach out and our hearts aspire.
Holy Spirit, Holy Spirit,
Holy Spirit, we welcome you.

Holy Spirit, we welcome you.
Holy Spirit, we welcome you.
Let the breeze of your presence blow,
that your children here might truly know
how to move in the Spirit's flow.
Holy Spirit, Holy Spirit,
Holy Spirit, we welcome you.

Holy Spirit, we welcome you.
Holy Spirit, we welcome you.
Please accomplish in me today
some new work of loving grace, I pray;
unreservedly have your way.
Holy Spirit, Holy Spirit,
Holy Spirit, we welcome you.

Chris Bowater
Copyright © 1986 Sovereign Lifestyle Music Ltd

155

HOW CAN I BE FREE FROM SIN?

Lead me to the cross of Jesus.
From the guilt, the power, the pain?
Lead me to the cross of Jesus.
There's no other way,
no price that I could pay;
simply to the cross I cling.
This is all I need, this is all I plead,
that his blood was shed for me.

How can I know peace within?
Lead me to the cross of Jesus.
Sing a song of joy again!
Lead me to the cross of Jesus.
Flowing from above, all-forgiving love
from the Father's heart to me!
What a gift of grace, his own righteousness
clothing me in purity!

How can I live day by day?
Lead me to the cross of Jesus.
Following his narrow way,
lead me to the cross of Jesus.

Graham Kendrick & Steve Thompson
Copyright © 1991 Make Way Music

155a Reconciled
Colossians 1:15

For God was pleased to have all his
fullness dwell in him, and through him
to reconcile to himself all things,
whether things on earth or things in heaven,
by making peace through his blood,
shed on the cross.

156
HOW DEEP THE FATHER'S LOVE FOR US
how vast beyond all measure,
that he should give his only Son
to make a wretch his treasure.
How great the pain of searing loss
the Father turns his face away,
as wounds which mar the chosen One
bring many sons to glory.

Behold the man upon a cross,
my sin upon his shoulders;
ashamed, I hear my mocking voice
call out among the scoffers.
It was my sin that held him there
until it was accomplished;
his dying breath has brought me life
I know that it is finished.

I will not boast in anything,
no gifts, no power, no wisdom;
but I will boast in Jesus Christ,
his death and resurrection.
Why should I gain from his reward?
I cannot give an answer;
but this I know with all my heart
his wounds have paid my ransom.

Stuart Townend
Copyright © 1995 Kingsway's Thankyou Music

157
HOW GOOD AND PLEASANT
it is when we all live in unity
refreshing as dew at the dawn
like rare anointing oil upon the head.

It's so good, so good
when we live together
in peace and harmony;
it's so good, so good
when we live together in his love.

How deep are the rivers that run
when we are one in Jesus
and share with the Father and Son
the blessings of his everlasting life.

Graham Kendrick
Copyright © 1995 Make Way Music

158
HOW LOVELY IS THY DWELLING PLACE
O Lord of hosts,
my soul longs and yearns for your courts,
and my heart and flesh sing for joy
to the living God.
One day in your presence
is far better to me than gold,
or to live my whole life somewhere else;
and I would rather be
a doorkeeper in your house
than to take my fate upon myself.

You are my sun and my shield,
you are my lover from the start,
and the highway to your city
runs through my heart.

Author unknown

159
HOW LOVELY IS YOUR DWELLING PLACE
O Lord Almighty.
My soul longs and even faints for you.
For here my heart is satisfied,
within your presence.
I sing beneath the shadow of your wings.

Better is one day in your courts,
better is one day in your house,
better is one day in your courts
than thousands elsewhere.
(Repeat)

One thing I ask and I would seek;
to see your beauty,
to find you in the place your glory dwells.

continued over...

35

My heart and flesh cry out
for you, the living God;
your Spirit's water for my soul.
I've tasted and I've seen,
come once again to me;
I will draw near to you, I will draw near to you.

Matt Redman
Copyright © 1995 Kingsway's Thankyou Music

160
HOW WONDERFUL, HOW GLORIOUS
is the love of God,
bringing healing, forgiveness,
wonderful love.

Let celebration echo through this land;
we bring reconciliation,
we bring hope to every man.

We proclaim the kingdom
of our God is here;
come and join the heavenly anthem,
ringing loud and ringing clear:

Listen to the music
as his praises fill the air;
with joy and with gladness
tell the people everywhere:

Dave Bilbrough
Copyright © 1994 Kingsway's Thankyou Music

161
HOW LOVELY ON THE MOUNTAINS
are the feet of him
who brings good news, good news,
proclaiming peace, announcing news of happiness,
our God reigns, our God reigns.

Our God reigns, our God reigns,
our God reigns, our God reigns.

You watchmen lift your voices joyfully as one,
shout for your King, your King.
See eye to eye the Lord restoring Zion:
your God reigns, your God reigns!

Waste places of Jerusalem break forth with joy,
we are redeemed, redeemed.
The Lord has saved and comforted his people:
your God reigns, your God reigns!

Ends of the earth, see the salvation of your God,
Jesus is Lord, is Lord.
Before the nations he has bared his holy arm:
your God reigns, your God reigns!

Leonard E. Smith Jnr
Copyright © 1974, 1978 Kingsway's Thankyou Music.

161a   A prayer of thanksgiving

Blessed are you, Lord our God.
How sweet are your words to the taste,
sweeter than honey to the mouth.
How precious are your commands for our
life, more than the finest gold in our hands.
How marvellous is your will for the world,
unending is your love for the nations.
Our voices shall sing of your promises
and our lips declare your praise
for ever and ever.
Amen.

From Common Worship:
Services and Prayers for the Church of England.

162
HOW PRECIOUS, O LORD
is your unfailing love,
we find refuge in the shadow of your wings.
We feast, Lord Jesus,
on the abundance of your house
and drink from your river of delights.
With you is the fountain of life,
in your light we see light.
With you is the fountain of life,
in your light we see light.

Phil Rogers
Copyright © 1982 Kingsway's Thankyou Music

162a   The Lord's unfailing love
Psalm 36:7

How priceless is your unfailing love!
Both high and low among men
find refuge in the shadow of your wings.

163
I AM A NEW CREATION
no more in condemnation,
here in the grace of God I stand.
My heart is overflowing,
my love just keeps on growing,
here in the grace of God I stand.

And I will praise you Lord,
yes, I will praise you Lord,
and I will sing of all that you have done.

A joy that knows no limit,
a lightness in my spirit,
here in the grace of God I stand.

Dave Bilbrough
Copyright © 1983 Kingsway's Thankyou Music

164

I AM THE BREAD OF LIFE

he who comes to me shall not hunger,
he who believes in me shall not thirst.
No one can come to me
unless the Father draw him.

And I will raise him up,
and I will raise him up,
and I will raise him up on the last day.

The bread that I will give
is my flesh for the life of the world,
and he who eats of this bread,
he shall live for ever, he shall live for ever.

Unless you eat of the flesh of the Son of Man
and drink of his blood, and drink of his blood,
you shall not have life within you.

I am the resurrection, I am the life,
he who believes in me
even if he die, he shall live for ever.

Yes, Lord, we believe that you are the Christ,
the Son of God who has come into the world.

S. Suzanne Toolan
Copyright © 1971 G.I.A Publications Inc.

165

I AM YOURS

and you are mine,
friend to me for all of time.

And all I have now I give to you;
and all I want now
is to be pure, pure like you.

I'm not afraid of earthly things,
for I am safe with you my King.

David Gate
Copyright © 1997 Kingsway's Thankyou Music

166

I BELIEVE IN JESUS

I believe he is the Son of God.
I believe he died and rose again,
I believe he paid for us all.

(Men) *And I believe he's here now,*
(Women) *I believe that he is here,*
(All) *standing in our midst.*

(Men) *Here with the power to heal now,*
(Women) *with the power to heal,*
(All) *and the grace to forgive.*

I believe in you, Lord;
I believe you are the Son of God.
I believe you died and rose again,
I believe you paid for us all.

Marc Nelson. Copyright © 1987
Mercy/Vineyard Publishing admin by CopyCare

166a   Blessings in Christ
Ephesians 1:3-6

Praise be to the God and Father of our
Lord Jesus Christ, who has blessed us in the
heavenly realms with every spiritual blessing
in Christ. For he chose us in him before the
creation of the world to be holy and blameless
in his sight.

In love he predestined us to be adopted as his
sons through Jesus Christ, in accordance with
his pleasure and will – to the praise of his
glorious grace, which he has freely given us
in the One he loves.

167

I BELIEVE THERE IS A GOD IN HEAVEN

who paid the price for all my sin;
shed his blood to open up the way
for me to walk with him.
Gave his life upon a cross,
took the punishment for us,
offered up himself in love, Jesus, Jesus.

'It is finished' was his cry;
not even death could now deny
the Son of God exalted high, Jesus, Jesus, Jesus.

Dave Bilbrough
Copyright © 1991 Kingsway's Thankyou Music

168

(OH) I COULD SING UNENDING SONGS

of how you saved my soul.
Well, I could dance a thousand miles
because of your great love.

My heart is bursting Lord, to tell of all you've done,
of how you changed my life and wiped away the past.
I wanna shout it out, from every roof top sing,
for now I know that God is for me, not against me.

Everybody's singing now, 'cause we're so happy!
Everybody's dancing now, 'cause we're so happy!
If only we could see your face,
and see you smiling over us,
and unseen angels celebrate, for joy is in this place!

Martin Smith. Copyright © 1994
Curious? Music UK/Adm. by Kingsway's Thankyou Music

169

I DON'T KNOW WHY

I can't see how
your precious blood could cleanse me now;
when all this time I've lived a lie,
with no excuse, no alibi.

All I know is I find mercy;
all my shame you take from me.
All I know, your cross has power,
and the blood you shed cleanses me.

It's way beyond what I can see,
how anyone could die for me.
So undeserved, this precious grace;
you've won my heart, I'll seek your face.

Noel & Tricia Richards & Wayne Drain
Copyright © 1998 Kingsway's Thankyou Music

170

I GET SO EXCITED LORD

every time I realise
I'm forgiven, I'm forgiven.
Jesus, Lord, you've done it all,
you've paid the price:
I'm forgiven, I'm forgiven.

Hallelujah, Lord,
my heart just fills with praise;
my feet start dancing, my hands rise up,
and my lips they bless your name.
I'm forgiven, I'm forgiven,
I'm forgiven. I'm forgiven,
I'm forgiven, I'm forgiven.

Living in your presence, Lord,
is life itself:
I'm forgiven, I'm forgiven.
With the past behind, grace for today
and a hope to come,
I'm forgiven, I'm forgiven.

Mick Ray
Copyright © 1978 Kingsway's Thankyou Music

171

I GIVE YOU ALL THE HONOUR

and praise that's due your name,
for you are the King of glory,
the creator of all things.

And I worship you,
I give my life to you,
I fall down on my knees.
Yes, I worship you,
I give my life to you,
I fall down on my knees.

As your Spirit moves upon me now
you meet my deepest need,
and I lift my hands up to your throne,
your mercy I've received.

You have broken chains that bound me,
you've set this captive free;
I will lift my voice to praise your name
for all eternity.

Carl Tuttle. Copyright © 1982
Mercy/Vineyard Publishing admin by CopyCare

172

I HEAR THE SOUND OF RUSTLING

in the leaves of the trees,
the Spirit of the Lord has come down on the earth.
The church that seemed in slumber
 has now risen from its knees,
and dry bones are responding
 with the fruits of new birth.
Oh, this is now a time for declaration,
the word will go to all men everywhere;
the church is here for healing of the nations,
behold the day of Jesus drawing near.

My tongue will be the pen of a ready writer,
and what the Father gives to me I'll sing;
I only want to be his breath,
I only want to glorify the King.

And all around the world
 the body waits expectantly,
the promise of the Father is now ready to fall.
The watchmen on the tower
 all exhort us to prepare,
and the church responds
 – a people who will answer the call.
And this is not a phase which is passing;
it's the start of an age that is to come.
And where is the wise man and the scoffer?
Before the face of Jesus they are dumb.

A body now prepared by God and ready for war,
the prompting of the Spirit
 is our word of command.
We rise, a mighty army,
 at the bidding of the Lord,
the devils see and fear, for their time is at hand.
And children of the Lord hear our commission
that we should love and serve our God as one.
The Spirit won't be hindered by division
in the perfect work that Jesus has begun.

Ronnie Wilson
Copyright © 1979 Kingsway's Thankyou Music

173

I KNOW A PLACE, A WONDERFUL PLACE,

where accused and condemned
find mercy and grace.
Where the wrongs we have done,
and the wrongs done to us
were nailed there with him (you)
there on the cross.

(Men)   At the cross,
(Women) At the cross,
(All)   he (you) died for my sin.
(Men)   At the cross,
(Women) At the cross,
(All)   he (you) gave us life again.

Randy & Terry Butler. Copyright © 1993
Mercy/Vineyard Publishing admin by CopyCare

174

I JUST WANT TO PRAISE YOU

lift my hands and say: 'I love you.'
You are everything to me,
and I exalt your holy name on high.
I just want to praise you,
lift my hands and say: 'I love you.'
You are everything to me,
and I exalt your holy name,
I exalt your holy name,
I exalt your holy name on high.

Arthur Tannous. Copyright © 1984, 1987
Acts Music/Kingsway's Thankyou Music

175

I LIFT MY EYES TO THE QUIET HILLS

in the press of a busy day;
as green hills stand in a dusty land,
so God is my strength and stay.

I lift my eyes to the quiet hills,
to a calm that is mine to share;
secure and still in the Father's will,
and kept by the Father's care.

I lift my eyes to the quiet hills,
with a prayer as I turn to sleep;
by day, by night,
through the dark and light,
my Shepherd will guard his sheep.

I lift my eyes to the quiet hills,
and my heart to the Father's throne;
in all my ways to the end of days,
the Lord will preserve his own.

Timothy Dudley-Smith
Copyright © 1968 Timothy Dudley-Smith

176

I LIFT MY EYES UP

to the mountains,
where does my help come from?
My help comes from you, maker of heaven,
creator of the earth.

O, how I need you, Lord,
you are my only hope;
you're my only prayer.
So I will wait for you
to come and rescue me,
come and give me life.

Brian Doerksen. Copyright © 1990
Mercy/Vineyard Publishing admin by CopyCare

177

I LIFT MY HANDS

to the coming King,
to the great I AM, to you I sing,
for you're the one
who reigns within my heart.

And I will serve no foreign god,
or any other treasure;
you are my heart's desire,
Spirit without measure.
Unto your name I will bring my sacrifice.

Andre Kempen. Copyright © 1989
Kempen Music/Kingsway's Thankyou Music.

178

I LIVE

I live because he is risen,
I live, I live with power over sin.
I live, I live because he is risen,
I live, I live to worship him.

Thank you Jesus, thank you Jesus,
because you're alive,
because you're alive,
because you're alive I live.

Rich Cook. Copyright © 1976 J.T. Benson Pub. Co.
Rights for UK and Eire administered by U.N. Music Publishing

179

I LOVE YOU LORD

and I lift my voice
to worship you, O my soul rejoice.
Take joy, my King, in what you hear,
may it be a sweet, sweet sound in your ear.
(Let me...)

Laurie Klein. Copyright © 1978, 1980
House of Mercy Music/Maranatha! Music admin. by CopyCare

180

I SEE THE LORD

seated on the throne, exalted:
and the train of his robe fills the temple with glory:
the whole earth is filled, the whole earth is filled,
the whole earth is filled with your glory.

Holy, holy, holy, holy,
yes, holy is the Lord.
Holy, holy, holy, holy,
yes, holy is the Lord of lords.

181

I SING A SIMPLE SONG OF LOVE

to my Saviour, to my Jesus.
I'm grateful for the things you've done,
my loving Saviour, oh precious Jesus.
My heart is glad that you've called me your own;
there's no place I'd rather be,

(Than) in your arms of love,
in your arms of love,
holding me still, holding me near
in your arms of love.

182

I SING PRAISES TO YOUR NAME

O Lord, praises to your name, O Lord,
for your name is great and greatly to be praised.
I sing praises to your name, O Lord,
praises to your name, O Lord,
for your name is great and greatly to be praised.

I give glory to your name...

183

I STAND AMAZED IN THE PRESENCE

of Jesus the Nazarene,
and wonder how he could love me,
a sinner, condemned, unclean.

How marvellous! How wonderful!
And my song shall ever be:
how marvellous! How wonderful!
Is my Saviour's love for me!

For me it was in the garden he prayed,
'Not my will, but thine':
he had no tears for his own griefs,
but sweat drops of blood for mine.

In pity angels beheld him,
and came from the world of light
to comfort him in the sorrows
he bore for my soul that night.

He took my sins and my sorrows,
he made them his very own;
he bore the burden of Calvary,
and suffered and died alone.

When with the ransomed in glory
his face I at last shall see,
'twill be my joy through the ages
to sing of his love for me.

184

I STAND AMAZED WHEN I REALISE

your love for me
is beyond all measure.
Lord, I can't deny
your love for me is great.

It's as high, high as the heavens above,
such is the depth of your love
toward those who fear you.
O Lord, far as the east is from west,
you have removed my transgressions.
You make my life brand new:
Father, I love you.

Your love is higher, high as the heavens.
Your love is deeper,
deeper than the deepest ocean.
Your love is stronger,
stronger than the powers of darkness.
Your love is sweeter, sweeter than wine.

185

I WALK BY FAITH

each step by faith,
to live by faith,
I put my trust in you.
(Repeat)

Every step I take is a step of faith;
no weapon formed against me shall prosper.
And every prayer I make is a prayer of
faith; and if my God is for me,
then who can be against me?

185a   Grow in God
2 Peter 1:5-7

For this very reason, make every effort
to add to your faith, goodness;
and to goodness, knowledge;
and to knowledge, self-control;
and to self-control, perseverance;
and to perseverance, godliness;
and to godliness, brotherly kindness;
and to brotherly kindness, love.

186
I WANT TO BE OUT OF MY DEPTH
in your love, feeling your arms so strong around me.
Out of my depth in your love,
out of my depth in you.
(Repeat)

Learning to let you lead, putting all trust in you;
deeper into your arms, surrounded by you.

Things I have held so tight, made my security;
give me the strength I need to simply let go.

186a   Where your treasure is
Luke 12:32-34

'Do not be afraid, little flock, for your Father
has been pleased to give you the kingdom.
Sell your possessions and give to the poor.
Provide purses for yourselves that will
not wear out, a treasure in heaven that
will not be exhausted, where no thief
comes near and no moth destroys.
For where your treasure is,
there your heart will be also.'

187
I WANT TO SERVE THE PURPOSE OF GOD
in my generation.
I want to serve the purpose of God
    while I am alive.
I want to give my life
    for something that will last forever.
Oh, l delight, I delight to do your will.

What is on your heart?
Tell me what to do;
Let me know your will
and I will follow you.
(Repeat)

I want to build with silver and gold
    in my generation.
I want to build with silver and gold
    while I am alive.
I want to give my life
    for something that will last forever.
Oh, l delight, I delight to do your will.

I want to see the kingdom of God
    in my generation.
I want to see the kingdom of God
    while I am alive.
I want to live my life
    for something that will last forever.
Oh, I delight, I delight to do your will.

I want to see the Lord come again
    in my generation.
I want to see the Lord come again
    while I am alive.
I want to give my life
    for something that will last forever
Oh, I delight, I delight to do your will.

188
I WANT TO WALK WITH JESUS CHRIST
all the days I live of this life on earth;
to give to him complete control
of body and of soul.

Follow him, follow him, yield your life to him,
he has conquered death, he is King of kings;
accept the joy which he gives to those
who yield their lives to him.

I want to learn to speak to him,
to pray to him, confess my sin;
to open my life and let him in,
for joy will then be mine:

I want to learn to speak of him,
my life must show that he lives in me;
my deeds, my thoughts, my words must speak
all of his love for me:

I want to learn to read his word,
for this is how I know the way
to live my life as pleases him,
in holiness and joy:

O Holy Spirit of the Lord,
enter now into this heart of mine;
take full control of my selfish will,
and make me wholly thine:

189

I WANT TO WORSHIP THE LORD

with all of my heart,
give him my all and not just a part.
Lift up my hands to the King of kings,
praise him in everything.

Robert Cameron. Copyright © 1986
Word's Spirit of Praise Music, admin. by CopyCare Ltd

190

I WAS ONCE IN DARKNESS

now my eyes can see,
I was lost but Jesus sought and found me.
O what love he offers,
O what peace he gives,
I will sing forever more, he lives.

Hallelujah Jesus! Hallelujah Lord!
Hallelujah Father, I am shielded by his word.
I will live forever, I will never die,
I will rise up to meet him in the sky.

Joan Parsons
Copyright © 1978 Kingsway's Thankyou Music

191

I WILL ENTER HIS GATES

with thanksgiving in my heart,
I will enter his courts with praise;
I will say this is the day that the Lord has made,
I will rejoice for he has made me glad.

He has made me glad,
he has made me glad,
I will rejoice for he has made me glad.
(Repeat)

Leona Von Brethorst
Copyright © 1976/1983 Maranatha! Music admin. by CopyCare

192

I WILL BUILD MY CHURCH

(Women) I will build my church
(Men) and the gates of hell
(Women) and the gates of hell
(Men) shall not prevail
(Women) shall not prevail
(All) against it.
(Repeat)

So you powers in the heavens above, bow down!
And you powers on the earth below, bow down!
And acknowledge that Jesus, Jesus, Jesus is Lord,
is Lord.

Graham Kendrick
Copyright © 1988 Make Way Music

193

I WILL DANCE

I will sing, to be mad for my King.
Nothing, Lord, is hindering
the passion in my soul.
(Repeat)

And I'll become even more undignified than this.
(Some would say it's foolishness but)
I'll become even more undignified than this.

Na, na, na, na, na, na! Hey!
Na, na, na, na, na, na! Hey!

Matt Redman
Copyright © 1995 Kingsway's Thankyou Music

193a   Praise the Lord!
Psalm 150

Praise the Lord.

Praise God in his sanctuary;
    praise him in his mighty heavens.
Praise him for his acts of power;
    praise him for his surpassing greatness.
Praise him with the sounding of the
    trumpet, praise him with the harp and lyre,
praise him with tambourine and dancing,
    praise him with the strings and flute,
praise him with the clash of cymbals,
    praise him with resounding cymbals.

Let everything that has breath
    praise the Lord.

Praise the Lord.

194

I WILL GIVE THANKS TO THEE

O Lord, among the people,
I will sing praises to thee among the nations.
For thy steadfast love is great,
is great to the heavens,
and thy faithfulness, thy faithfulness to the clouds.

Be exalted, O God, above the heavens.
Let thy glory be over all the earth.
(Repeat)

(Last time only)
Be exalted, O God, above the heavens.
Let thy glory be over all the earth.
Be exalted, O God, above the heavens.
Let thy glory, let thy glory,
let thy glory be over all the earth.

Brent Chambers. Copyright © 1977 Scripture in Song,
a division of Integrity Music/Adm. by Kingsway's Thankyou Music

195

I WILL OFFER UP MY LIFE

In spirit and truth,
pouring out the oil of love as my worship to you.
In surrender I must give my every part;
Lord, receive the sacrifice of a broken heart.

Jesus, what can I give, what can I bring
to so faithful a friend, to so loving a King?
Saviour, what can be said, what can be sung
as a praise of your name
for the things you have done?
Oh, my words could not tell, not even in part,
of the debt of love that is owed
by this thankful heart.

You deserve my every breath
for you've paid the great cost;
giving up your life to death, even death on a cross.
You took all my shame away, there defeated my sin,
opened up the gates of heaven,
and have beckoned me in.

Matt Redman
Copyright © 1994 Kingsway's Thankyou Music

196

I WILL SEEK YOUR FACE

O Lord; I will seek your face, O Lord.
I will seek your face, O Lord;
I will seek your face, O Lord.

Lord, how awesome is your presence;
who can stand in your light?
Those who by your grace and mercy
are made holy in your sight.

I will dwell in your presence
all the days of my life;
there to gaze upon your glory,
and to worship only you.

Noel & Tricia Richards
Copyright © 1990 Kingsway's Thankyou Music

196a   You are my God
Hosea 2:23

I will plant her for myself in the land;
I will show my love to the one I called
'Not my loved one'.
I will say to those called
'Not my people',
'You are my people';
and they will say,
'You are my God.'

197

I WILL SING THE WONDROUS STORY

of the Christ who died for me;
how he left his home in glory
for the cross on Calvary.
I was lost but Jesus found me,
found the sheep that went astray;
threw his loving arms around me,
drew me back into his way.

I was bruised but Jesus healed me,
faint was I from many a fall;
sight was gone, and fears possessed me,
but he freed me from them all.
Days of darkness still come o'er me;
sorrow's paths I often tread,
but the Saviour still is with me,
by his hand I'm safely led.

He will keep me till the river
rolls its waters at my feet,
then he'll bear me safely over,
all my joys in him complete.
yes, I'll sing the wondrous story
of the Christ who died for me;
sing it with the saints in glory,
gathered by the crystal sea.

Rowland H Prichard (1811-87) & Francis H Rawley (1854-1952)
Words Copyright © HarperCollins Religious admin. by CopyCare

198

I WILL SING UNTO THE LORD

as long as I live,
I will sing praise to my God while I have my being.
My meditation of him shall be sweet,
I will be glad, I will be glad in the Lord.

Bless thou the Lord, O my soul, praise ye the Lord.
(Repeat x3)

Donya Brockway. Copyright © 1972
BMG Gospel Music Inc. admin by CopyCare

199

I WILL SPEAK OUT

for those who have no voices.
I will stand up for the rights of all the oppressed;
I will speak truth and justice, I'll defend the poor
and the needy, I will lift up the weak in Jesus' name.

I will speak out for those who have no choices,
I will cry out for those who live without love;
I will show God's compassion to the crushed and
broken in spirit, I will lift up the weak in Jesus' name.

D. Bankhead/R. Goudie/S. Rinaldi/S. Bassett
© 1990 Word's Spirit of Praise Music admin. by CopyCare

200
I WILL WORSHIP
(I will worship)
with all of my heart (with all of my heart).
I will praise you (I will praise you)
with all of my strength (all my strength).
I will seek you (I will seek you)
all of my days (all of my days)
I will follow (I will follow)
all of your ways (all your ways).

I will give you all my worship,
I will give you all my praise.
you alone I long to worship,
you alone are worthy of my praise.

I will bow down (I will bow down)
hail you as King (hail you as King).
I will serve you (I will serve you)
give you everything (give you everything).
I will lift up (I will lift up)
my eyes to your throne (my eyes to your throne),
I will trust you (I will trust you)
I will trust you alone (trust you alone).

David Ruis. Copyright © 1993
Shade Tree Music/Maranatha! Music admin. by CopyCare

201
I WILL LOVE YOU FOR THE CROSS
and I will love you for the cost;
Man of sufferings, bringer of my peace,
you came into a world of shame,
and paid the price we could not pay:
death that brought me life,
blood that brought me home.
Death that brought me life,
blood that brought me home.

And I love you for the cross,
I'm overwhelmed by the mystery.
I love you for the cost
that Jesus you would do this for me.
When you were broken, you were beaten,
you were punished, I go free.
When you were wounded and rejected,
in your mercy I am healed.

Jesus Christ, the sinner's friend;
does this kindness know no bounds?
With your precious blood you have purchased me.
O the mystery of the cross,
you were punished, you were crushed;
but that punishment has become my peace.
Yes that punishment has become my peace.

Matt & Beth Redman
Copyright © 1998 Kingsway's Thankyou Music

202
I WORSHIP YOU, ALMIGHTY GOD
there is none like you.
I worship you, O Prince of Peace,
that is what I love to do.
I give you praise, for you are my righteousness.
I worship you, Almighty God, there is none like you.

Sondra Corbett. Copyright © 1983
Integrity's Hosanna! Music/Adm. Kingsway's Thankyou Music

203
IF I WERE A BUTTERFLY
I'd thank you, Lord, for giving me wings.
And if I were a robin in a tree,
I'd thank you, Lord, that I could sing.
And if I were a fish in the sea,
I'd wiggle my tail and I'd giggle with glee;
but I just thank you, Father, for making me 'me'.

For you gave me a heart and you gave me a smile,
you gave me Jesus and you made me your child,
and I just thank you, Father, for making me 'me'.

If I were an elephant,
I'd thank you, Lord, by raising my trunk.
And if I were a kangaroo,
you know I'd hop right up to you.
And if I were an octopus,
I'd thank you, Lord, for my fine looks;
but I just thank you, Father, for making me 'me'.

If I were a wiggily worm,
I'd thank you, Lord, that I could squirm.
And if I were a billy goat,
I'd thank you, Lord, for my strong throat.
And if I were a fuzzy-wuzzy bear,
I'd thank you, Lord, for my fuzzy-wuzzy hair;
but I just thank you, Father, for making me 'me'.

Brian Howard
Copyright © 1974, 1975 Mission Hills Music admin by CopyCare

204
IMMANUEL, O IMMANUEL
bowed in awe I worship at your feet,
and sing Immanuel, God is with us;
sharing my humanness, my shame,
feeling my weaknesses, my pain,
taking the punishment, the blame, Immanuel.

And now my words cannot explain,
all that my heart cannot contain,
how great are the glories of your name, Immanuel.

... Immanuel (x3)

Graham Kendrick
Copyright © 1988 Make Way Music

204a   The Lord's Prayer

Our Father in heaven,
hallowed be your name,
your kingdom come, your will be done,
on earth as in heaven.
Give us today our daily bread.
Forgive us our sins
as we forgive those who sin against us.
Lead us not into temptation
but deliver us from evil.
For the kingdom, the power,
and the glory are yours now and for ever.
Amen.

From Common Worship:
Services and Prayers for the Church of England.

205

I'M ACCEPTED

I'm forgiven,
I am fathered by the true and living God.
I'm accepted, no condemnation,
I am loved by the true and living God.
There's no guilt or fear as I draw near
to the Saviour and Creator of the world.
There is joy and peace as I release
my worship to you, O Lord

Rob Hayward
Copyright © 1985 Kingsway's Thankyou Music

206

I'M SPECIAL

because God has loved me,
for he gave the best thing that he had to save me;
his own son Jesus, crucified to take the blame
for all the bad things I have done.

Thank you Jesus, thank you Lord,
for loving me so much.
I know I don't deserve anything.
Help me feel your love right now,
to know deep in my heart
that I'm your special friend.

Graham Kendrick
Copyright © 1986 Kingsway's Thankyou Music

207

IN EVERY CIRCUMSTANCE OF LIFE

you are with me, glorious Father.
And I have put my trust in you,
that I may know the glorious hope
to which I'm called.

And by the power that works in me,
you've raised me up and set me free;
and now in every circumstance
I'll prove your love without a doubt,
your joy shall be my strength (x2)

David Fellingham
Copyright © 1994 Kingsway's Thankyou Music

208

IN HEAVENLY ARMOUR

we'll enter the land, the battle belongs to the Lord.
No weapon that's fashioned against us will stand,
the battle belongs to the Lord.

And we sing glory, honour,
power and strength to the Lord.
We sing glory, honour,
power and strength to the Lord.

When the power of darkness comes in like a flood,
the battle belongs to the Lord.
He's raised up a standard, the power of his blood,
the battle belongs to the Lord.

When your enemy presses in hard, do not fear,
the battle belongs to the Lord.
Take courage, my friend, your redemption is near.
The battle belongs to the Lord.

Jamie Owens-Collins
Copyright © 1984 Fairhill Music admin by CopyCare

208a   The armour of God
Ephesians 6:10-13

Finally, be strong in the Lord and in his
mighty power. Put on the full armour of God
so that you can take your stand against the
devil's schemes. For our struggle is not against
flesh and blood, but against the rulers, against
the authorities, against the powers of this dark
world and against the spiritual forces of evil in
the heavenly realms. Therefore put on the full
armour of God, so that when the day of evil
comes, you may be able to stand your ground,
and after you have done everything, to stand.

209

IN MOMENTS LIKE THESE

I sing out a song, I sing out a love song to Jesus.
In moments like these I lift up my hands,
I lift up my hands to the Lord.

Singing, I love you, Lord (x2)
singing, I love you, Lord, I love you.

David Graham
Copyright © 1980 C.A. Music admin by CopyCare

210

IN MY LIFE, LORD
be glorified, be glorified.
In my life, Lord, be glorified today.

In your church, Lord,
be glorified, be glorified.
In your church, Lord, be glorified today.

211

INTO THE DARKNESS OF THIS WORLD
into the shadows of the night;
into this loveless place you came,
lightened our burdens, eased our pain,
and made these hearts your home.
Into the darkness once again,
O come, Lord Jesus, come.

Come with your love to make us whole,
come with your light to lead us on,
driving the darkness far from our souls:
O come, Lord Jesus, come.

Into the longing of our souls,
into these heavy hearts of stone,
shine on us now your piercing light,
order our lives and souls aright,
by grace and love unknown,
until in you our hearts unite
O come, Lord Jesus, come.

O holy child, Emmanuel,
hope of the ages, God with us,
visit again this broken place,
till all the earth declares your praise
and your great mercies own.
Now let your love be born in us,
O come, Lord Jesus, come.

(Last chorus)
Come in your glory, take your place,
Jesus, the name above all names,
we long to see you face to face,
O come, Lord Jesus, come.

212

IN THE TOMB SO COLD THEY LAID HIM
death its victim claimed.
Powers of hell, they could not hold him;
back to life he came!

Christ is risen! (Christ is risen!)
Death has been conquered. (Death has been conquered)
Christ is risen! (Christ is risen!)
He shall reign for ever.

Hell had spent its fury on him,
left him crucified.
Yet, by blood, he boldly conquered,
sin and death defied.

Now the fear of death is broken,
love has won the crown.
Prisoners of the darkness
listen, walls are tumbling down.

Raised from death to heaven ascending,
love's exalted King.
Let his song of joy, unending,
through the nations ring!

213

ISN'T HE BEAUTIFUL
beautiful isn't he?
Prince of Peace, Son of God, isn't he?
Isn't he wonderful, wonderful isn't he?
Counsellor, Almighty God,
isn't he, isn't he, isn't he?

Yes, you are beautiful...

214

IS ANYONE THIRSTY
anyone?
Is anyone thirsty?
Is anyone thirsty, anyone?
Is anyone thirsty?
Jesus said:
'Let them come to me and drink,
let them come to me.'

O, let the living waters flow,
O, let the living waters flow,
let the river of your Spirit
flow through me.
(Repeat)
Flow through me.

Let the living waters flow.
Let the living waters flow.
Let the living waters flow.
Let the living waters flow.

215
IS IT TRUE TODAY
that when people pray,
cloudless skies will break,
kings and queens will shake?
Yes it's true, and I believe it, I'm living for you.

Well it's true today that when people pray
we'll see dead men rise, and the blind set free.
Yes it's true and I believe it, I'm living for you.

I'm gonna be a history maker in this land.
I'm gonna be a speaker of truth to all mankind.
I'm gonna stand, I'm gonna run into your arms,
into your arms again,
into your arms, into your arms again.

Yes it's true today that when people stand
with the fire of God and the truth in hand,
we'll see miracles, we'll see angels sing,
we'll see broken hearts making history.
Yes it's true, and we believe it, we're living for you.

Martin Smith. Copyright © 1996
Curious? Music UK/Adm. by Kingsway's Thankyou Music

216
IT IS THE CRY OF MY HEART
to follow you.
It is the cry of my heart to be close to you.
It is the cry of my heart to follow
all of the days of my life.
(Repeat)

Teach me your holy ways, O Lord,
so I can walk in your truth.
Teach me your holy ways, O Lord,
and make me wholly devoted to you.

Open my eyes so I can see
the wonderful things that you do.
Open my heart up more and more
and make it wholly devoted to you.

(Last time chorus)
... all of the days of my life. (x2)

Terry Butler. Copyright © 1991
Mercy/Vineyard Publishing/Adm. by CopyCare

217
IT'S RISING UP
from coast to coast,
from north to south, and east to west;
the cry of hearts that love your name,
which with one voice we will proclaim.

The former things have taken place,
can this be the new day of praise?

A heavenly song that comes to birth,
and reaches out to all the earth.
Oh, let the cry to nations ring,
that all may come and all may sing:

'Holy is the Lord.' (Every heart sing:)
'Holy is the Lord.' (With one voice sing:)
'Holy is the Lord.' (Every heart sing:)
'Holy is the Lord.'

And we have heard the Lion's roar,
that speaks of heaven's love and power.
Is this the time, is this the call
that ushers in your kingdom rule?
Oh, let the cry to nations ring,
that all may come and all may sing:

'Jesus is alive!' (Every heart sing:)...

Matt Redman & Martin Smith
Copyright © 1995 Kingsway's Thankyou Music

218
IT'S YOUR BLOOD
that cleanses me, it's your blood that gives me life.
It's your blood that took my place
in redeeming sacrifice, and washes me
whiter than the snow, than the snow.
My Jesus, God's precious sacrifice.

Michael Christ. Copyright © 1985
Mercy/Vineyard Publishing admin by CopyCare

219
JEHOVAH JIREH, MY PROVIDER
his grace is sufficient for me, for me, for me.
Jehovah Jireh, my provider,
his grace is sufficient for me.

My God shall supply all my needs
according to his riches in glory;
he will give his angels charge over me,
Jehovah Jireh cares for me, for me, for me,
Jehovah Jireh cares for me.

Merla Watson. Copyright © 1974
Lorenz Publishing Co./MCA Music Publishing

220
JESUS, ALL FOR JESUS
all I am and have and ever hope to be.
(Repeat)

All of my ambitions hopes and plans
I surrender these in to your hands.
(Repeat)

For it's only in your will that I am free (Repeat)

Robin Mark & Jennifer Atkinson
Copyright © 1991 Word's Spirit of Praise Music admin by CopyCare

221
JESUS, AT YOUR NAME
we bow the knee.
Jesus, at your name we bow the knee.
Jesus, at your name we bow the knee
and acknowledge you as Lord.
You are the Christ, you are the Lord;
through your Spirit in our lives
we know who you are.

Chris Bowater
Copyright © 1982 Sovereign Lifestyle Music

222
JESUS, BE THE CENTRE
be my source, be my light, Jesus.

Jesus, be the centre,
be my hope, be my song, Jesus.

Be the fire in my heart,
be the wind in these sails,
be the reason that I live; Jesus, Jesus.

Jesus, be my vision,
be my path, be my guide, Jesus.

(Repeat verse 1)

Michael Frye. Copyright © 1999
Vineyard Songs (UK/Eire) admin. by CopyCare

222a A prayer for healing

Be with us, Spirit of God
nothing can separate us from your love.
Breathe on us, breath of God;
fill us with your saving power
Speak in us, wisdom of God;
bring strength, healing and peace.
The Lord is here.
His Spirit is with us.

The Peace

Peace to you from God our Father
who hears our cry.
Peace from his Son Jesus Christ whose
death brings healing.
Peace from the Holy Spirit who gives us
life and strength.
The peace of the Lord be always with you
and also with you.

From Common Worship:
Services and Prayers for the Church of England.

223
JESUS CHRIST, I THINK
UPON YOUR SACRIFICE
you became nothing, poured out to death.
Many times I've wondered at your gift of life,
and I'm in that place once again,
and I'm in that place once again.

And once again I look upon
the cross where you died,
I'm humbled by your mercy
and I'm broken inside.
Once again I thank you,
once again I pour out my life.

Now you are exalted to the highest place,
King of the heavens, where one day I'll bow.
But for now, I marvel at this saving grace,
and I'm full of praise once again.
I'm full of praise once again.

And once again I look upon...

... thank you for the cross, thank you for the cross,
thank you for the cross, my friend.
(Repeat)

Matt Redman
Copyright © 1995 Kingsway's Thankyou Music

224
JESUS CHRIST IS THE LORD OF ALL
Lord of all the earth.
Jesus Christ is the Lord of all, Lord of all the earth.
(Repeat)

Only one God over the nations,
only one Lord of all.
In no other name is there salvation,
Jesus is Lord of all.

Jesus Christ is Lord of all.
Jesus Christ is Lord of all.
Jesus Christ is Lord of all.
Jesus Christ is Lord of all.

Steve Israel & Gerrit Gustafson. Copyright © 1988
Integrity's Hosanna! Music/Adm. by Kingsway's Thankyou Music

224a   One God
1 Corinthians 8:6

... yet for us there is but one God, the Father,
from whom all things came and for whom we
live; and there is but one Lord, Jesus Christ,
through whom all things came and through
whom we live.

225

JESUS, GOD'S RIGHTEOUSNESS REVEALED
the Son of Man, the Son of God -
his kingdom comes;
Jesus, redemption's sacrifice,
now glorified, now justified:
his kingdom comes.

And this kingdom will know no end,
and its glory shall know no bounds;
for the majesty and power
of this kingdom's King has come.
And this kingdom's reign, and this kingdom's rule,
and this kingdom's power and authority:
Jesus, God's righteousness revealed.

Jesus, the expression of God's love,
the grace of God,
the Word of God revealed to us.
Jesus, God's holiness displayed,
now glorified, now justified,
his kingdom comes.

Geoff Bullock. Copyright © 1995
Maranatha! Music/Word Music admin. by CopyCare

226

JESUS, HOW LOVELY YOU ARE
you are so gentle, so pure and kind.
You shine as the morning star,
Jesus, how lovely you are.

Hallelujah, Jesus is my Lord and King;
hallelujah, Jesus is my everything.

Hallelujah, Jesus died and rose again;
hallelujah, Jesus forgave all my sin.

Hallelujah, Jesus is meek and lowly;
hallelujah, Jesus is pure and holy.

Hallelujah, Jesus is the Bridegroom;
hallelujah, Jesus will take his bride soon.

Dave Bolton
Copyright © 1975 Kingsway's Thankyou Music

227

JESUS, I LOVE YOU
I worship and adore you.
Jesus, I love you,
Lord, I glorify your name.

You are mighty, O Lord,
the Ancient of Days.
Your love stands forever,
unfailing your ways.

You are reigning on high,
exalted King.
Your throne is eternal,
you are Lord over all.

Judith Butler & Paul Hemingway
Copyright © 1996 Paul Hemingway

228

JESUS IS KING
and I will extol him,
give him the glory, and honour his name.
He reigns on high, enthroned in the heavens,
Word of the Father, exalted for us.

We have a hope that is steadfast and certain,
gone through the curtain and touching the throne.
We have a priest who is there interceding,
pouring his grace on our lives day by day.

We come to him, our priest and apostle,
clothed in his glory and bearing his name,
laying our lives with gladness before him;
filled with his Spirit we worship the King.

O holy One, our hearts do adore you;
thrilled with your goodness we give you our praise.
Angels in light with worship surround him,
Jesus, our Saviour, forever the same.

Wendy Churchill
Copyright © 1982 Word's Spirit of Praise Music/Adm. by CopyCare

229

JESUS IS LORD!
Creation's voice proclaims it,
for by his power each tree and flower
was planned and made.
Jesus is Lord! The universe declares it,
sun, moon and stars in heaven cry, 'Jesus is Lord!'

Jesus is Lord! Jesus is Lord!
Praise him with hallelujahs
for Jesus is Lord!

Jesus is Lord! Yet from his throne eternal
in flesh he came
to die in pain on Calvary's tree.
Jesus is Lord! From him all life proceeding,
yet gave his life a ransom
thus setting us free.

Jesus is Lord! O'er sin the mighty conqueror,
from death he rose,
and all his foes shall own his name.
Jesus is Lord! God sent his Holy Spirit
to show by works of power that Jesus is Lord.

David J. Mansell
Copyright © 1982 Word's Spirit of Praise Music admin by CopyCare

230

JESUS IS THE NAME WE HONOUR

Jesus is the name we praise.
Majestic name above all other names,
the highest heaven and earth proclaim
that Jesus is our God.

We will glorify, we will lift him high,
we will give him honour and praise.
We will glorify, we will lift him high,
we will give him honour and praise.

Jesus is the name we worship;
Jesus is the name we trust.
He is the King above all other kings,
let all creation stand and sing
that Jesus is our God.

Jesus is the Father's splendour;
Jesus is the Father's joy.
He will return to reign in majesty,
and every eye at last will see
that Jesus is our God.

Phil Lawson Johnston
Copyright © 1991 Kingsway's Thankyou Music

231

JESUS, JESUS, HEALER, SAVIOUR

strong Deliverer,
how I love you,
how I love you.

David Fellingham
Copyright © 1998 Kingsway's Thankyou Music

232

JESUS, JESUS, HOLY AND ANOINTED ONE

Jesus. Jesus, Jesus,
risen and exalted One, Jesus.

Your name is like honey on my lips,
your Spirit like water to my soul.
Your word is a lamp unto my feet;
Jesus I love you, I love you.

John Barnett. Copyright © 1988
Mercy/Vineyard Publishing admin by CopyCare

233

JESUS, KING OF KINGS

we worship and adore you.
Jesus, Lord of heaven and earth,
we bow down at your feet.
Father, we bring to you our worship;
your sovereign will be done,
on earth your kingdom come,
through Jesus Christ, your only Son.

Jesus, Sovereign Lord,
we worship and adore you.
Jesus, name above all names,
we bow down at your feet.
Father, we offer you our worship;
your sovereign will be done,
on earth your kingdom come,
through Jesus Christ, your only Son.

Jesus, Light of the world,
we worship and adore you.
Jesus, Lord Emmanuel,
we bow down at your feet.
Father, for your delight we worship;
your sovereign will be done,
on earth your kingdom come,
through Jesus Christ, your only Son.

Chris Rolinson
Copyright © 1988 Kingsway's Thankyou Music

234

JESUS, LOVER OF MY SOUL

all consuming fire is in your gaze.
Jesus, I want you to know
I will follow you all my days.
For no one else in history is like you,
and history itself belongs to you.
Alpha and Omega, you have loved me,
and I will share eternity with you.

It's all about you, Jesus,
and all this is for you,
for your glory and your fame.
It's not about me,
as if you should do things my way;
you alone are God,
and I surrender to your ways.

Paul Oakley
Copyright © 1995 Kingsway's Thankyou Music.

235

JESUS, LOVER OF MY SOUL,
JESUS, I WILL NEVER LET YOU GO

you've taken me from the miry clay,
you've set my feet upon the rock
and now I know:

I love you, I need you,
though my world will fall,
I'll never let you go;
my Saviour, my closest friend,
I will worship you until the very end.

John Ezzy, Daniel Grul & Stephen McPherson.
Copyright © 1992 John Ezzy, Daniel Grul & Stephen McPherson/
Hillsong Publishing/Kingsway's Thankyou Music

236
JESUS, LOVER OF MY SOUL, LET ME TO THY BOSOM FLY

while the nearer waters roll,
while the tempest still is high;
hide me, O my Saviour, hide,
till the storm of life is past;
safe into the haven guide,
O receive my soul at last.

Other refuge have I none,
hangs my helpless soul on thee;
Leave, ah, leave me not alone,
still support and comfort me.
All my trust on thee is stayed,
all my help from thee I bring;
cover my defenceless head
with the shadow of thy wing.

Thou, O Christ, art all I want;
more than all in thee I find;
raise the fallen, cheer the faint,
heal the sick, and lead the blind.
Just and holy is thy name,
I am all unrighteousness;
false and full of sin I am,
thou art full of truth and grace.

Plenteous grace with thee is found,
grace to cover all my sin;
let the healing streams abound,
make and keep me pure within.
Thou of life the fountain art;
freely let me take of thee;
spring thou up within my heart, rise to all eternity.

Charles Wesley (1707-88)

237
JESUS, JESUS, JESUS

your love has melted my heart.
(Repeat)

Chris Bowater
Copyright © 1979, 1991 Sovereign Lifestyle Music

238
JESUS, NAME ABOVE ALL NAMES

beautiful Saviour, glorious Lord;
Emmanuel, God is with us,
blessèd Redeemer, living Word.

Naida Hearn. Copyright © 1974, 1979 Scripture in Song,
a division of Integrity Music/Kingsway's Thankyou Music

239
JESUS PUT THIS SONG INTO OUR HEARTS

Jesus put this song into our hearts,
it's a song of joy no one can take away,
Jesus put this song into our hearts.

Jesus taught us how to live in harmony,
Jesus taught us how to live in harmony,
different faces, different races, he made us one,
Jesus taught us how to live in harmony.

Jesus taught us how to be a family,
Jesus taught us how to be a family,
loving one another with the love that he gives,
Jesus taught us how to be a family.

Jesus turned our sorrow into dancing,
Jesus turned our sorrow into dancing,
changed our tears of sadness into rivers of joy,
Jesus turned our sorrow into a dance.

Graham Kendrick
Copyright © 1986 Kingsway's Thankyou Music

240
JESUS, RESTORE TO US AGAIN

the gospel of your holy name,
that comes with power, not words alone,
owned, signed and sealed from heaven's throne.
Spirit and word in one agreed;
the promise to the power wed.

The word is near, here in our mouths
and in our hearts, the word of faith;
proclaim it on the Spirit's breath: Jesus!

Your word, O Lord, eternal stands,
fixed and unchanging in the heavens;
the Word made flesh, to earth come down
to heal our world with nail-pierced hands.
Among us here you lived and breathed,
you are the message we received.

Spirit of truth, lead us, we pray
into all truth as we obey,
and as God's will we gladly choose,
your ancient powers again will prove
Christ's teaching truly comes from God,
he is indeed the living Word.

continued over...

Upon the heights of this great land
with Moses and Elijah stand.
Reveal your glory once again,
show us your face, declare your name.
Prophets and law, in you complete
where promises and power meet.

Grant us in this decisive hour
to know the scriptures and the power;
the knowledge in experience proved,
the power that moves and works by love.
May word and works join hands as one,
the word go forth, the Spirit come.

Graham Kendrick
Copyright © 1992 Make Way Music

241
JESUS SHALL TAKE
THE HIGHEST HONOUR
Jesus shall take the highest praise.
Let all earth join heaven in exalting
the name which is above all other names.

Let's bow the knee in humble adoration,
for at his name every knee must bow.
Let every tongue confess
he is Christ, God's only Son;
Sovereign Lord, we give you glory now.

For all honour
and blessing and power
belongs to you, belongs to you.
For all honour
and blessing and power
belongs to you, belongs to you.
Lord Jesus Christ,
Son of the living God.

Chris Bowater
Copyright © 1988 Sovereign Lifestyle Music

242
JESUS TAKE ME AS I AM
I can come no other way.
Take me deeper into you,
make my flesh life melt away.
Make me like a precious stone,
crystal clear and finely honed,
life of Jesus shining through,
giving glory back to you.

Dave Bryant
Copyright © 1978 Kingsway's Thankyou Music

243
JESUS STAND AMONG US
at the meeting of our lives;
be our sweet agreement
at the meeting of our eyes.
O Jesus, we love you, so we gather here;
join our hearts in unity and take away our fear.

So to you we're gathering
out of each and every land;
Christ the love between us
at the joining of our hands.
O Jesus, we love you, so we gather here;
join our hearts in unity and take away our fear.

(Optional verse for Communion:)

Jesus, stand among us
at the breaking of the bread;
join us as one body
as we worship you, our head.
O Jesus, we love you, so we gather here;
join our hearts in unity and take away our fear.

Graham Kendrick
Copyright © 1977 Kingsway's Thankyou Music

244
JESUS, WHAT A BEAUTIFUL NAME
Son of God, Son of Man,
Lamb that was slain.
Joy and peace, strength and hope,
grace that blows all fear away.
Jesus, what a beautiful name.

Jesus, what a beautiful name.
Truth revealed, my future sealed, healed my pain.
Love and freedom, life and warmth,
grace that blows all fear away.
Jesus, what a beautiful name.

Jesus, what a beautiful name.
Rescued my soul, my stronghold,
lifts me from shame.
Forgiveness, security, power and love,
grace that blows all fear away.
Jesus, what a beautiful name.

Tanya Riches. Copyright © 1995
Tanya Riches/Hillsong Publishing/Kingsway's Thankyou Music

245
JESUS, WE CELEBRATE YOUR VICTORY
Jesus, we revel in your love.
Jesus, we rejoice, you've set us free;
Jesus, your death has brought us life.

It was for freedom that Christ has set us free,
no longer to be subject to a yoke of slavery;
so we're rejoicing in God's victory,
our hearts responding to his love.

His Spirit in us releases us from fear,
the way to him is open, with boldness we draw near;
and in his presence our problems disappear,
our hearts responding to his love.

John Gibson
Copyright © 1987 Kingsway's Thankyou Music

246
JESUS, WE ENTHRONE YOU
we proclaim you our King.
Standing here in the midst of us,
we raise you up with our praise.
And as we worship, build a throne,
and as we worship, build a throne,
and as we worship, build a throne:
come, Lord Jesus, and take your place.

Paul Kyle
Copyright © 1980 Kingsway's Thankyou Music

246a 'My Lord and my God!'
John 20:26b-29

... Jesus came and stood among them
and said, 'Peace be with you!'
Then he said to Thomas,
'Put your finger here; see my hands.
Reach out your hand and put it into my side.
Stop doubting and believe.'
Thomas said to him, 'My Lord and my God!'
Then Jesus told him,
'Because you have seen me, you have believed;
blessed are those who have not seen and yet
have believed.'

247
JESUS, YOU ARE CHANGING ME
by your Spirit you're making me like you.
Jesus, you're transforming me,
that your loveliness may be seen in all I do.
You are the potter and I am the clay,
help me to be willing to let you have your way.
Jesus, you are changing me,
as I let you reign supreme within my heart.

Marilyn Baker. Copyright © 1981
Word's Spirit of Praise Music admin by CopyCare

247a The Potter's hand
Jeremiah 18:5-6

Then the word of the Lord came to me:
'O house of Israel, can I not do with
you as this potter does?' declares the Lord.
'Like clay in the hand of the potter,
so are you in my hand, O house of Israel.'

248
JESUS, YOU ARE THE RADIANCE
of the Father's glory,
you are the Son, the appointed heir,
through whom all things are made.
You are the One who sustains
all things by your powerful word.
You have purified us from sin,
you are exalted, O Lord,
exalted, O Lord, to the right hand of God.

(Last time) Crowned with glory,
crowned with honour, we worship you.

David Fellingham
Copyright © 1985 Kingsway's Thankyou Music

248a Jesus, the radiance
of God's glory
Hebrews 1:3

The Son is the radiance of God's glory
and the exact representation of his being,
sustaining all things by his powerful word.

249
JUBILATE, EVERYBODY
serve the Lord in all your ways,
and come before his presence singing,
enter now his courts with praise.
For the Lord our God is gracious,
and his mercy's everlasting.
Jubilate, jubilate, jubilate Deo.

Fred Dunn
Copyright © 1977, 1980 Kingsway's Thankyou Music

250

JUST LIKE YOU PROMISED

you've come;
just like you told us, you're here,
and our desire is that you know
we love you, we worship you,
we welcome you here.

Patty Kennedy. Copyright © 1982
Mercy/Vineyard Publishing/Adm. by CopyCare

251

JUST LET ME SAY
HOW MUCH I LOVE YOU

let me speak of your mercy and grace
just let me live in the shadow of your beauty
let me see you face to face.
And the earth will shake as your word goes forth
and the heavens can tremble and fall,
but let me say how much I love you
O my Saviour, my Lord and friend.

Just let me hear your finest whispers
as you gently call my name
and let me see your power and your glory
let me feel your Spirit's flame.
Let me find you in the desert
'til this sand is holy ground
and I am found completely surrendered to you,
my Lord and friend.

Just let me say how much I love you
with all my heart I long for you
for I'm caught in the passion of knowing
this endless love I've found in you.
And the depth of grace, the forgiveness found,
to be called a child of God
just makes me say how much I love you,
O my Saviour, my Lord and friend.

Geoff Bullock. Copyright © 1993
Word Music/Maranatha! Music admin. by CopyCare

251a   We wait on the Lord
Psalm 123:1-2

I lift my eyes to you,
to you whose throne is in heaven.
As the eyes of slaves
look to the hand of their master,
as the eyes of a maid
look to the hand of her mistress,
so our eyes look to the Lord our God
till he shows us his mercy.

252

KING OF KINGS, MAJESTY

God of heaven living in me.
Gentle Saviour, closest friend,
strong Deliverer, beginning and end.
All within me falls at your throne.

Your majesty, I can but bow,
I lay my all before you now.
In royal robes I don't deserve
I live to serve your majesty.

Earth and heaven worship you.
Love eternal, faithful and true,
who bought the nations, ransomed souls,
brought this sinner near to your throne.
All within me cries out in praise.

Jarrod Cooper
Copyright © 1996 Sovereign Lifestyle Music

252a   Prayers

Almighty God, who called your Church
to bear witness that you were in Christ
reconciling the world to yourself:
help us to proclaim the good news
of your love,
that all who hear it may be drawn to you;
through him who was lifted up on the cross,
and reigns with you in the unity of the
Holy Spirit, one God, now and for ever.
Amen

Collect of the Thirteenth Sunday after Trinity.
A Collect for mission and evangelism

Almighty and everlasting God,
by whose Spirit the whole body of the
Church is governed and sanctified:
hear our prayer which we offer for all your
faithful people, that in their vocation and
ministry they may serve you in holiness
and truth to the glory of your name;
through our Lord and Saviour Jesus Christ,
who is alive and reigns with you
in the unity of the Holy Spirit,
one God, now and for ever.
Amen

Collect of the Fifth Sunday after Trinity.
A Collect for the ministry of all Christian people.

From Common Worship:
Services and Prayers for the Church of England.

253
LAMB OF GOD
holy One, Jesus Christ, Son of God,
lifted up willingly to die,
that I the guilty one may know
the blood once shed, still freely flowing,
still cleansing, still healing.

I exalt you, Jesus my sacrifice;
I exalt you, my Redeemer and my Lord.
I exalt you, worthy Lamb of God,
and in honour I bow down before your throne.

253a   Sacrificed for us
Isaiah 53:5

But he was pierced for our transgressions,
he was crushed for our iniquities;
the punishment that brought us peace was
upon him, and by his wounds we are healed.

254
LED LIKE A LAMB
to the slaughter in silence and shame,
there on your back you carried a world
of violence and pain.
Bleeding, dying, bleeding, dying.

You're alive, you're alive,
you have risen, alleluia!
And the power and the glory is given,
alleluia, Jesus, to you.

At break of dawn, poor Mary,
still weeping she came,
when through her grief she heard your voice
now speaking her name.
Mary, master, Mary, master!

At the right hand of the Father
now seated on high
you have begun your eternal reign
of justice and joy.
Glory, glory, glory, glory.

255
LET EVERYTHING THAT
everything that,
everything that has breath
praise the Lord.
(Repeat)

Praise you in the morning,
praise you in the evening,
praise you when I'm young
and when I'm old.
Praise you when I'm laughing,
praise you when I'm grieving,
praise you every season of the soul.

If we could see how much you're worth,
your power, your might, your endless love,
then surely we would never cease to praise:

Praise you in the heavens,
joining with the angels,
praising you forever and a day.
Praise you on the earth now,
joining with creation,
calling all the nations to your praise.

If they could see how much you're worth,
your power, your might, your endless love,
then surely they would never cease to praise:

256
LET IT BE TO ME
according to your word;
let it be to me according to your word.
I am your servant, no rights shall I demand.
Let it be to me, let it be to me,
let it be to me according to your word.

257
LET ME HAVE MY WAY AMONG YOU
do not strive, do not strive.
Let me have my way among you,
do not strive, do not strive.
For mine is the power and the glory
for ever and ever the same.
Let me have my way among you,
do not strive, do not strive.

We'll let you have your way among us,
we'll not strive, we'll not strive.
We'll let you have your way among us,
we'll not strive, we'll not strive.
For yours is the power and the glory
for ever and ever the same.
We'll let you have your way among us,
we'll not strive, we'll not strive.

continued over...

Let my peace rule within your hearts,
do not strive, do not strive.
Let my peace rule within your hearts,
do not strive, do not strive.
For mine is the power and the glory,
for ever and ever the same.
Let my peace rule within your hearts,
do not strive, do not strive.

We'll let your peace rule within our hearts,
we'll not strive, we'll not strive.
We'll let your peace rule within our hearts,
we'll not strive, we'll not strive.
For yours is the power and the glory,
for ever and ever the same.
We'll let your peace rule within our hearts,
we'll not strive, we'll not strive.

Graham Kendrick
Copyright © 1977 Kingsway's Thankyou Music

258
LET OUR PRAISE TO YOU BE AS INCENSE
let our praise to you be as pillars of your throne.
Let our praise to you be as incense,
as we come before you and worship you alone.

As we see you in your splendour,
as we gaze upon your majesty,
as we join the hosts of angels
and proclaim together your holiness.

Holy, holy, holy,
holy is the Lord.
Holy, holy, holy
holy is the Lord.

Brent Chambers. Copyright © 1979 Scripture in Song,
a division of Integrity Music/Adm. by Kingsway's Thankyou Music

258a   The glory of the Lord
2 Chronicles 5:13-14

The trumpeters and singers joined in unison,
as with one voice, to give praise and thanks
to the Lord.
Accompanied by trumpets, cymbals and
other instruments, they raised their voices
in praise to the Lord and sang:
'He is good; his love endures for ever.'
Then the temple of the Lord was filled with a
cloud, and the priests could not perform their
service because of the cloud, for the glory of
the Lord filled the temple of God.

259
LET THERE BE JOY
let there be peace
let there be power, let there be praise.
Let there be joy, joy in the Holy Ghost.

It was for freedom that we were set free,
let ev'ry mountain be cast to the sea.
Let there be joy, joy in the Holy Ghost.

We will declare it to the heavens,
the righteousness of God in which we stand.
We will proclaim it to the nations;
ev'ry eye shall see, ev'ry ear shall hear,
ev'ry heart will understand.

Bruce Napier
Copyright © 1998 Ironspiration Music

260
LET THERE BE LOVE
shared among us,
let there be love in our eyes;
may now your love sweep this nation,
cause us, O Lord, to arise.
Give us a fresh understanding
of brotherly love that is real;
let there be love shared among us,
let there be love.

Dave Bilbrough
Copyright © 1979 Kingsway's Thankyou Music

261
LET YOUR LIVING WATER FLOW
over my soul.
Let your Holy Spirit come and take control
of every situation that has troubled my mind.
All my cares and burdens on to you I roll.

Jesus, Jesus, Jesus.
Father, Father, Father.
Spirit, Spirit, Spirit.

Come now, Holy Spirit, and take control.
Hold me in your loving arms and make me whole.
Wipe away all doubt and fear and take my pride,
draw me to your love and keep me by your side.

Give your life to Jesus, let him fill your soul.
Let him take you in his arms and make you whole.
As you give your life to him he'll set you free.
You will live and reign with him eternally.

John Watson
Copyright © 1986 Ampelos Music admin by CopyCare

262

LIFT UP YOUR HEADS

to the coming King;
bow before him and adore him, sing
to his majesty, let your praises be
pure and holy, giving glory
to the King of kings.

Steven Fry. Copyright © 1974
BMG Gospel Music Inc/Adm. by CopyCare

263

LIVING UNDER THE SHADOW OF HIS WING

we find security.
Standing in his presence we will bring
our worship, worship, worship to the King.

Bowed in adoration at his feet
we dwell in harmony.
Voices joined together that repeat,
worthy, worthy, worthy is the Lamb.

Heart to heart embracing in his love
reveals his purity.
Soaring in my spirit like a dove,
holy, holy, holy is the Lord.

David J. Hadden & Bob Silvester. Copyright © 1983
Restoration Music admin. by Sovereign Music UK

264

LIGHT HAS DAWNED

that ever shall blaze;
darkness flees away.
Christ the light has shone in our hearts,
turning night to day.

We proclaim him King of kings,
we lift high his name.
Heaven and earth shall bow at his feet
when he comes to reign.

Saviour of the world is he,
heaven's King come down.
Judgement, love and mercy meet
at his thorny crown.

Life has sprung from hearts of stone,
by the Spirit's breath.
Hell shall let her captives go,
life has conquered death.

Blood has flowed that cleanses from sin,
God his love has proved.
Men may mock and demons may rage,
we shall not be moved!

Graham Kendrick
Copyright © 1988 Make Way Music

265

LORD, COME AND HEAL YOUR CHURCH

take our lives and cleanse with your fire.
Let your deliverance flow,
as we lift your name up higher.

We will draw near,
and surrender our fear;
lift our hands to proclaim
holy Father, you are here.

Spirit of God, come in
and release our hearts to praise you.
Make us whole, for
holy we'll become, and serve you.

Show us your power, we pray,
that we might share in your glory.
We shall arise and go
to proclaim your works most holy.

Chris Rolinson
Copyright © 1988 Kingsway's Thankyou Music

266

LORD, FOR THE YEARS

your love has kept and guided,
urged and inspired us, cheered us on our way,
sought us and saved us, pardoned and provided,
Lord of the years, we bring our thanks today.

Lord, for that word,
the word of life which fires us,
speaks to our hearts and sets our souls ablaze,
teaches and trains, rebukes us and inspires us:
Lord of the word, receive your people's praise.

Lord, for our land in this our generation,
spirits oppressed by pleasure, wealth and care:
for young and old, for commonwealth and nation,
Lord of our land, be pleased to hear our prayer.

Lord, for our world;
when we disown and doubt him,
loveless in strength, and comfortless in pain,
hungry and helpless, lost indeed without him:
Lord of the world, we pray that Christ may reign.

Lord for ourselves;
in living power remake us,
self on the cross and Christ upon the throne;
past put behind us, for the future take us:
Lord of our lives, to live for Christ alone.

Timothy Dudley-Smith & Michael Baughen
Words Copyright © Timothy Dudley-Smith

267
LORD, HOW MAJESTIC YOU ARE
my eyes meet your gaze
and my burden is lifted.
Your word is a lamp to my feet,
your hand swift to bless
and your banner a shield.

You are my everything,
you who made earth and sky and sea,
all that you've placed inside of me
calls out your name.

To you I bow,
the King who commands my every breath,
the Man who has conquered sin and death,
my Lord and my King, my everything!

Lord, how resplendent you are,
when I think of your heavens,
the work of your fingers –
what is man, that you are mindful of him?
Yet you've crowned him with glory
and caused him to reign!

Stuart Townend
Copyright © 1990 Kingsway's Thankyou Music

268
LORD, I AM NOT MY OWN
no longer my own,
living now for you,
and everything I think, all I say and do
is for you, my Lord.

Now taking up the cross,
walking on your paths,
holding out your truth,
running in this race, bowing every day,
all for you, my Lord.

And what I have vowed I will make good,
every promise made will be fulfilled,
till the day I die, every day I live
is for you, is for you, is for you,
is for you, is for you, is for you.

Earth has nothing I desire
that lives outside of you,
I'm consumed with you.
Treasures have no hold,
nothing else will do,
only you, my Lord.

And what I have vowed...

Matt Redman
Copyright © 1998 Kingsway's Thankyou Music

268a   Living for Jesus
2 Corinthians 4:8-10

We are hard pressed on every side, but
not crushed; perplexed, but not in despair;
persecuted, but not abandoned; struck down,
but not destroyed. We always carry around in
our body the death of Jesus, so that the life of
Jesus may also be revealed in our body.

269
LORD, I COME BEFORE
your throne of grace;
I find rest in your presence and fulness of joy.
In worship and wonder I behold your face,
singing what a faithful God have I.

What a faithful God have I,
what a faithful God.
What a faithful God have I,
faithful in every way.

Lord of mercy, you have heard my cry;
through the storm you're the beacon,
    my song in the night.
In the shelter of your wings, hear my heart's reply,
singing what a faithful God have I.

Lord all sovereign, granting peace from heaven,
let me comfort those who suffer
with the comfort you have given.
I will tell of your great love for as long as I live,
singing what a faithful God have I.

Robert & Dawn Critchley
Copyright © 1989 Kingsway's Thankyou Music

270
LORD, I COME TO YOU
let my heart be changed, renewed,
flowing from the grace that I found in you.
And Lord, I've come to know
the weaknesses I see in me
will be stripped away by the power of your love.

Hold me close, let your love surround me.
Bring me near, draw me to your side.
And as I wait I'll rise up like the eagle,
and I will soar with you, your Spirit leads me on
in the power of your love.

Lord, unveil my eyes, let me see you face to face,
the knowledge of your love as you live in me.
Lord, renew my mind
    as your will unfolds in my life,
in living every day by the power of your love.

Geoff Bullock. Copyright © 1992
Word Music/Maranatha! Music admin. by CopyCare

271

LORD, I LONG TO SEE YOU GLORIFIED

in everything I do;
all my heart-felt dreams I put aside,
to see your Spirit move with power in my life.

Jesus, Lord of all eternity,
your children rise in faith;
all the earth displays your glory,
and each word you speak
brings life to all who hear.

Lord of all, all of creation sings your praise
in heaven and earth.
Lord, we stand, hearts open wide,
be exalted.

(Last time chorus)
... be exalted, be exalted

272

LORD, I LIFT YOUR NAME ON HIGH

Lord, I love to sing your praises.
I'm so glad you're in my life;
I'm so glad you came to save us.

You came from heaven to earth to show the way,
from the earth to the cross, my debt to pay.
From the cross to the grave, from the grave to the sky,
Lord, I lift your name on high.

273

LORD JESUS CHRIST

you have come to us,
you are one with us, Mary's son.
Cleansing our souls from all their sin,
pouring your love and goodness in;
Jesus, our love for you we sing, living Lord.

(Optional communion verse:)
Lord Jesus Christ, now and every day,
teach us how to pray, Son of God.
You have commanded us to do
this in remembrance, Lord, of you:
into our lives your power breaks through,
living Lord.

Lord Jesus Christ, you have come to us,
born as one of us, Mary's son.
Led out to die on Calvary,
risen from death to set us free,
living Lord Jesus, help us see you are Lord.

Lord Jesus Christ, we would come to you,
live our lives for you, Son of God.
All your commands we know are true,
your many gifts will make us new,
into our lives your power breaks through,
living Lord.

274

LORD, LET YOUR GLORY FALL

as on that ancient day;
songs of enduring love,
and then your glory came.
And as a sign to you that we would love the same
our hearts will sing that song:
God, let your glory come.

You are good, you are good,
and you love endures,
(Repeat x2)
today.

Voices in unison, giving you thanks and praise,
joined by the instruments,
and then your glory came.
Your presence like a cloud upon that ancient day,
the priests were overwhelmed
because your glory came.

A sacrifice was made, and then your fire came;
they knelt upon the ground
and with one voice they praised.
(Repeat)

275

LORD, MY HEART CRIES OUT

'glory to the King'.
My greatest love in life, I hand you everything:
'glory, glory', I hear the angels sing.

Open my ears, let me hear your voice,
to know that sweet sound, oh, my soul rejoice:
'glory, glory', I hear the angels sing.

You're the Father to the fatherless,
the answer to my dreams.
I see you crowned in righteousness,
we cry, 'glory to the King'.
Comforter to the lonely, the lifter of my head.
I see you veiled in majesty;
we cry, 'glory, glory',
we cry, 'Glory to the King'.

276
LORD, MAKE ME AN INSTRUMENT
an instrument of worship;
I lift up my hands in your name.
Lord make me an instrument,
an instrument of worship;
I lift up my hands in your name.

I'll sing you a love song,
a love song of worship,
I'll lift up my hands in your name.
I'll sing you a love song,
a love song to Jesus,
I'll lift up my hands in your name.

For we are a symphony,
a symphony of worship;
we lift up our hands in your name.
For we are a symphony,
a symphony of worship;
we lift up our hands in your name.

We'll sing you a love song,
a love song of worship,
we'll lift up our hands in your name.
We'll sing you a love song,
a love song to Jesus,
we'll lift up our hands in your name.

Author Unknown
Copyright © 1977 Zion Song Music/Adm. by CopyCare

277
LORD OF ALL HOPEFULNESS
Lord of all joy,
whose trust, ever child-like,
no cares could destroy;
be there at our waking,
and give us, we pray,
your bliss in our hearts, Lord,
at the break of the day.

Lord of all eagerness, Lord of all faith,
whose strong hands were skilled
at the plane and the lathe;
be there at our labours,
and give us, we pray,
your strength in our hearts, Lord,
at the noon of the day.

Lord of all kindliness, Lord of all grace,
your hands swift to welcome,
your arms to embrace;
be there at our homing,
and give us, we pray,
your love in our hearts, Lord,
at the eve of the day.

Lord of all gentleness, Lord of all calm,
whose voice is contentment,
whose presence is balm;
be there at our sleeping,
and give us, we pray,
your peace in our hearts, Lord,
at the end of the day.

Words: Jan Struther (1901-53) from 'Enlarged Songs of Praise'.
By permission of Oxford University Press

278
LORD OF LORDS, KING OF KINGS
Maker of heaven and earth and all good things,
we give you glory.
Lord Jehovah, Son of Man
precious Prince of Peace and the great I AM,
we give you glory.

Glory to God! Glory to God!
Glory to God Almighty, in the highest!

Lord, you're righteous in all your ways.
We bless your holy name
and we will give you praise,
we give you glory.
You reign forever in majesty,
we praise you and lift you up for eternity,
we give you glory.

Jessy Dixon, Randy Scruggs & John Thompson. Copyright © 1981
Whole Armor Publishing & Full Armor Publishing Companies
admin. By TKO Publishing Ltd

279
LORD, POUR OUT YOUR SPIRIT
on all the peoples of the earth;
let your sons and daughters
speak your words of prophecy.
Send us dreams and visions,
reveal the secrets of your heart;
Lord, our faith is rising,
let all heaven sound the coming of your day.

There's gonna be a great awakening,
there's gonna be a great revival in our land.
There's gonna be a great awakening,
and everyone who calls on Jesus, they will be saved.

Lord, pour out your Spirit
on all the nations of the world;
let them see your glory,
let them fall in reverent awe.
Show your mighty power,
shake the heavens and the earth;
Lord, the world is waiting,
let creation see the coming of your day.

R Goudie/D Bankhead/S Bassett. Copyright © 1993 Integrity's Hosanna!
Music/New Generation Music/adm. by Kingsway's Thankyou Music

280

LORD, THE LIGHT OF YOUR LOVE

is shining, in the midst of the darkness, shining;
Jesus, Light of the world, shine upon us,
set us free by the truth you now bring us,
shine on me, shine on me.

Shine, Jesus, shine,
fill this land with the Father's glory;
blaze, Spirit, blaze, set our hearts on fire.
Flow, river, flow,
flood the nations with grace and mercy;
send forth your word, Lord, and let there be light.

Lord, I come to your awesome presence,
from the shadows into your radiance;
by the blood I may enter your brightness,
search me, try me, consume all my darkness.
Shine on me, shine on me.

As we gaze on your kingly brightness
so our faces display your likeness.
Ever changing from glory to glory,
mirrored here may our lives tell your story.
Shine on me, shine on me.

Graham Kendrick
Copyright © 1987 Make Way Music

281

LORD, WE LONG FOR YOU

to move in power;
there's a hunger deep within our hearts,
to see healing in our nation.
Send your Spirit to revive us:

Heal our nation,
heal our nation,
heal our nation,
pour out your Spirit on this land.

Lord we hear your Spirit, coming closer,
a mighty wave to break upon our land,
bringing justice, and forgiveness.
God we cry to you, 'Revive us':

Trish Morgan, Ray Goudie, Ian Townend, Dave Bankhead
Copyright © 1986 Kingsway's Thankyou Music

282

LORD, YOU ARE
MORE PRECIOUS THAN SILVER

Lord, you are more costly than gold.
Lord, you are more beautiful than diamonds,
and nothing I desire compares with you.

Lynn DeShazo. Copyright © 1985
Integrity's Hosanna! Music/Adm. Kingsway's Thankyou Music

283

LORD, YOU HAVE MY HEART

and I will search for yours;
Jesus, take my life and lead me on.
Lord, you have my heart,
and I will search for yours;
let me be to you a sacrifice.

(Men)   And I will praise you, Lord.
(Women) I will praise you, Lord.
(Men)   And I will sing of love come down.
(Women) I will sing of love come down.)
(Men)   And as you show your face,
(Women) Show your face,
(All)   We'll see your glory here.

Martin Smith
Copyright © 1992 Kingsway's Thankyou Music

283a   Living sacrifices
Romans 12:1

Therefore, I urge you, brothers, in view
of God's mercy, to offer your bodies as
living sacrifices, holy and pleasing to God
this is your spiritual act of worship.

284

LORD, YOU ARE SO PRECIOUS TO ME

Lord, you are so precious to me
and I love you, yes, I love you,
because you first loved me.

Lord, you are so gracious to me,
Lord, you are so gracious to me,
and I love you, yes, I love you,
because you first loved me.

Graham Kendrick
Copyright © 1986 Kingsway's Thankyou Music

285

LOVE BEYOND MEASURE

mercy so free,
your endless resources
given to me.
Strength to the weary,
healing our lives,
your love beyond measure
has opened my eyes,
opened my eyes.

Dave Bilbrough
Copyright © 1984 Kingsway's Thankyou Music

286

LOVE DIVINE, ALL LOVES EXCELLING

joy of heaven to earth come down!
Fix in us thy humble dwelling,
all thy faithful mercies crown.
Jesus, thou art all compassion,
pure unbounded love thou art;
visit us with thy salvation,
enter every trembling heart.

Breathe, O breathe thy loving Spirit
into every troubled breast!
Let us all in thee inherit,
let us find thy promised rest.
Take away the love of sinning;
Alpha and Omega be;
end of faith, as its beginning,
set our hearts at liberty.

Come, Almighty to deliver,
let us all thy grace receive;
suddenly return, and never,
never more thy temples leave.
Thee we would be always blessing,
serve thee as thy hosts above,
pray, and praise thee without ceasing,
glory in thy perfect love.

Finish then thy new creation,
pure and spotless let us be;
let us see thy great salvation
perfectly restored in thee!
Changed from glory into glory,
till in heaven we take our place;
till we cast our crowns before thee,
lost in wonder, love and praise.

Charles Wesley (1707-88)

287

LOVE SONGS FROM HEAVEN

are filling the earth,
bringing great hope to all nations.
Evil has prospered, but truth is alive;
in this dark world the light still shines.

Nothing has silenced this gospel of Christ;
it echoes down through the ages.
Blood of the martyrs has made your church strong;
in this dark world the light still shines.

For you we live, and for you we may die;
through us may Jesus be seen.
For you alone we will offer our lives;
in this dark world our light will shine.

Let every nation be filled with your song:
this is the cry of your people.
We will not settle for anything less,
in this dark world our light must shine.

Noel & Tricia Richards
Copyright © 1996 Kingsway's Thankyou Music

288

MAJESTY

worship his majesty,
unto Jesus be glory, honour and praise.
Majesty, kingdom authority,
flows from his throne unto his own,
his anthem raise.

So exalt, lift up on high the name of Jesus,
magnify, come glorify Christ Jesus the King.
Majesty, worship his majesty,
Jesus who died, now glorified, King of all kings.

Jack W. Hayford. Copyright © 1976 Rocksmith Music
admin in UK by Leosong Copyright Service

288a   To us is given
Isaiah 9:6-7

For to us a child is born, to us a son is given,
and the government will be on his shoulders.
And he will be called Wonderful Counsellor,
Mighty God, Everlasting Father,
Prince of Peace. Of the increase of his
government and peace there will be no end.
He will reign on David's throne and over his
kingdom, establishing and upholding it with
justice and righteousness from that time on
and for ever. The zeal of the Lord Almighty
will accomplish this.

289

MAKE WAY, MAKE WAY

for Christ the King
in splendour arrives.
Fling wide the gates and welcome him
into your lives.

Make way! (Make way!)
Make way! (Make way!)
For the King of kings. (For the King of kings)
Make way! (Make way!)
Make way! (Make way!)
And let his kingdom in.

He comes the broken hearts to heal,
the prisoners to free.
The deaf shall hear, the lame shall dance,
the blind shall see.

And those who mourn with heavy hearts,
who weep and sigh;
with laughter, joy and royal crown he'll beautify.

We call you now to worship him as Lord of all.
To have no gods before him,
their thrones must fall!

290
MAY THE FRAGRANCE
of Jesus fill this place.
(Women) May the fragrance of Jesus fill this place.
(Men) May the fragrance of Jesus fill this place.
(Women) Lovely fragrance of Jesus,
(All) rising from the sacrifice of lives laid
down in adoration.

(Men) May the glory of Jesus fill his church.
(Women) May the glory of Jesus fill his church.
(Men) May the glory of Jesus fill his church.
(Women) Radiant glory of Jesus,
(All) shining from our faces as we gaze in
adoration.

(Men) May the beauty of Jesus fill my life.
(Women) May the beauty of Jesus fill my life.
(Men) May the beauty of Jesus fill my life.
(Women) Perfect beauty of Jesus,
(All) fill my thoughts, my words, my deeds,
my all I give in adoration.

291
MEEKNESS AND MAJESTY
manhood and deity,
in perfect harmony, the man who is God.
Lord of eternity dwells in humanity,
kneels in humility and washes our feet.

O what a mystery, meekness and majesty.
Bow down and worship
for this is your God, this is your God.

Father's pure radiance, perfect in innocence,
yet learns obedience to death on a cross.
Suffering to give us life,
conquering through sacrifice,
and as they crucify, prays: 'Father forgive.

Wisdom unsearchable, God the invisible,
love indestructible in frailty appears.
Lord of infinity, stooping so tenderly,
lifts our humanity to the heights of his throne.

292
MEN OF FAITH
rise up and sing
of the great and glorious King;
you are strong when you feel weak,
in your brokenness complete.

Shout to the north and the south,
sing to the east and the west:
Jesus is Saviour to all,
Lord of heaven and earth.

Rise up women of the truth,
stand and sing to broken hearts,
who can know the healing power
of our glorious King of love.

We've been through fire,
we've been through rain;
we've been refined by the power of his name.
We've fallen deeper in love with you,
you've burned the truth on our lips.

Shout to the north...

Rise up church with broken wings;
fill this place with songs again,
of our God who reigns on high:
by his grace again we'll fly.

Shout to the north...

(Last time chorus)
... Lord of heaven and earth (x3).

293
MIGHTY GOD
everlasting Father, wonderful Counsellor,
you're the Prince of Peace.
(Repeat)

You are Lord of heaven,
you are called Emmanuel;
God is now with us,
ever present to deliver.
You are God eternal, you are Lord of all the earth;
love has come to us, bringing us new birth.

A light to those in darkness,
and a guide to paths of peace;
love and mercy dawns,
grace, forgiveness and salvation.
Light for revelation, glory to your people;
Son of the Most High, God's love gift to all.

294
MIGHTY IS OUR GOD

mighty is our King;
mighty is our Lord,
ruler of everything.

Glory to our God,
Glory to our King;
Glory to our Lord,
ruler of everything.

His name is higher,
higher than any other name;
his power is greater,
for he has created everything.

294a Confession and Absolution

Leader   Lord God, our maker and our
         Redeemer, this is your world and
         we are your people:
         come among us and save us.
         We have wilfully misused your
         gifts of creation;
         Lord, be merciful:
All   **forgive us our sin.**

Leader   We have seen the ill-treatment
         of others and have not gone
         to their aid; Lord, be merciful:
All   **forgive us our sin.**

Leader   We have condoned evil and
         dishonesty and failed to strive
         for justice; Lord, be merciful:
All   **forgive us our sin.**

Leader   We have heard the good news of
         Christ, but have failed to share it
         with others; Lord, be merciful:
All   **forgive us our sin.**

Leader   We have not loved you with all
         our heart, nor our neighbours
         as ourselves; Lord, be merciful:
All   **forgive us our sin.**

May the God of all healing and forgiveness
draw us to himself, and cleanse us from
all our sins that we may behold the glory
of his Son, the Word made flesh,
Jesus Christ our Lord.
Amen

295
MORE LOVE (MORE LOVE)

More power (more power),
more of you in my life.
More love (more love),
More power (more power),
more of you in my life.

*And I will worship you with all of my heart,
and I will worship you with all of my mind,
and I will worship you with all of my strength,
for you are my Lord.*

*(Last time)
And I will seek your face with all of my heart,
and I will seek your face with all of my mind,
and I will seek your face with all of my strength,
for you are my Lord, you are my Lord.*

295a   God's love
1 John 4:16b-21

God is love. Whoever lives in love lives in
God, and God in him. In this way, love is
made complete among us so that we will have
confidence on the day of judgment, because
in this world we are like him. There is no
fear in love. But perfect love drives out fear,
because fear has to do with punishment. The
one who fears is not made perfect in love.

We love because he first loved us. If anyone
says, 'I love God,' yet hates his brother, he
is a liar. For anyone who does not
love his brother, whom he has seen,
cannot love God, whom he has not seen.
And he has given us this command:
Whoever loves God must also love his
brother.

296
MORE THAN OXYGEN

I need your love;
more than life-giving food
the hungry dream of.
More than an eloquent word
depends on the tongue;
more than a passionate song
needs to be sung.

*More than a word could ever say,
more than a song could ever convey;
I need you more than all of these things.
Father, I need you more.*

More than magnet and steel
are drawn to unite;
more that poets love words
to rhyme as they write.
More than comforting warmth
of sun in spring;
more than the eagle loves wind under its wings.

More than a blazing fire
on a winter's night;
more than tall evergreens
reach for the light.
More than the pounding waves
long for the shore;
more than these gifts you give, I love you more.

297

MORNING HAS BROKEN
like the first morning;
blackbird has spoken like the first bird.
Praise for the singing!
Praise for the morning!
Praise for them springing fresh from the word!

Sweet the rain's new fall
sunlit from heaven,
like the first dewfall on the first grass.
Praise for the sweetness
of the wet garden,
sprung in completeness where his feet pass.

Mine is the sunlight!
Mine is the morning
born of the one light Eden saw play!
Praise with elation,
praise every morning,
God's re-creation of the new day!

298

MY FIRST LOVE IS A BLAZING FIRE
I feel his powerful love in me.
For he has kindled a flame of passion,
and I will let it grow in me.
And in the night I will sing your praise, my love.
And in the morning I'll seek your face, my love.

And like a child I will dance in your presence,
Oh, let the joy of heaven pour down on me.
I still remember the first day I met you,
and I don't ever want to lose that fire, my first love.

My first love is a rushing river,
a waterfall that will never cease;

and in the torrent of tears and laughter,
I feel a healing power released.
And I will draw from your well of life, my love,
and in your grace I'll be satisfied, my love.

Restore the years of the church's slumber,
revive the fire that has grown so dim;
renew the love of those first encounters,
that we may come alive again.
And we will rise like the dawn
throughout the earth,
until the trumpet announces your return.

299

MY HEART IS FULL OF ADMIRATION
for you, my Lord, my God and King.
Your excellence my inspiration,
your words of grace have made my spirit sing.

All the glory, honour and power
belong to you, belong to you.
Jesus, Saviour, Anointed One,
I worship you, I worship you.

You love what's right and hate what's evil,
therefore your God sets you on high,
and on your head pours oil of gladness,
while fragrance fills your royal palaces.

Your throne, O God, will last forever,
justice will be your royal decree.
In majesty, ride out victorious,
for righteousness, truth and humility.

300

MY JESUS, MY SAVIOUR
Lord, there is none like you.
All of my days I want to praise
the wonders of your mighty love.
My comfort, my shelter,
tower of refuge and strength,
let every breath, all that I am,
never cease to worship you.

Shout to the Lord all the earth, let us sing
power and majesty, praise to the King.
Mountains bow down and the seas will roar
at the sound of your name.
I sing for joy at the work of your hands.
Forever I'll love you, forever I'll stand.
Nothing compares to the promise I have in you.

301
MY JESUS, MY LIFELINE
I need you more than I've ever known.
There's no one quite like you,
I'm crying out for your loving.

Oh Jesus, oh Jesus,
I've never known a love like this before.
Oh Jesus, oh Jesus,
accept this love I give to you,
It's all I can do.

I'm searching, I'm longing,
please meet me just as you want to.
I'll stand here to offer,
offer up this song of love to you.

Tim Hughes
Copyright © 1997 Kingsway's Thankyou Music

302
MY LIPS SHALL PRAISE YOU
my great Redeemer;
my heart will worship
Almighty Saviour.

You take all my guilt away,
turn the darkest night to brightest day,
you are the restorer of my soul.

Love that conquers every fear,
in the midst of trouble you draw near,
you are the restorer of my soul.

You're the source of happiness,
bringing peace when I am in distress,
you are the restorer of my soul.

Noel & Tricia Richards
Copyright © 1991 Kingsway's Thankyou Music

303
MY LIFE IS IN YOU, LORD
my strength is in you, Lord,
my hope is in you, Lord,
In you, it's in you.
(Repeat)

(Last time)
In you.

I will praise you with all of my life;
I will praise you with all of my strength.
With all of my life,
with all of my strength;
all of my hope is in you.

Daniel Gardner. Copyright © 1986 Integrity's Hosanna! Music/
Adm. By Kingsway's Thankyou Music

303a   God will bless you
Deuteronomy 30:15-16

See, I set before you today life and prosperity,
death and destruction. For I command you
today to love the Lord your God, to walk in
his ways, and to keep his commands, decrees
and laws; then you will live and increase, and
the Lord your God will bless you in the land
you are entering to possess.

304
MY LORD, WHAT LOVE IS THIS
that pays so dearly,
that I, the guilty one, may go free!

Amazing love, O what sacrifice,
the Son of God given for me.
My debt he pays, and my death he dies,
that I might live, that I might live.

(Last time only)
That I might live!

And so they watched him die,
despised, rejected;
but oh, the blood he shed flowed for me!

And now, this love of Christ
shall flow like rivers;
come wash your guilt away, live again!

Graham Kendrick
Copyright © 1989 Make Way Music

305
MY PEACE
I give unto you,
it's a peace that the world cannot give,
It's a peace that the world cannot understand:
peace to know, peace to live,
my peace I give unto you.

My joy...

My love...

Keith Routledge
Copyright © 1975 Sovereign Music UK

306
NAME OF ALL MAJESTY
fathomless mystery,
King of the ages
by angels adored;
power and authority,
splendour and dignity,
bow to his mastery, Jesus is Lord!

Child of our destiny,
God from eternity,
love of the Father
on sinners outpoured;
see now what God has done,
sending his only Son,
Christ the belovèd One,
Jesus is Lord!

Saviour of Calvary,
costliest victory,
darkness defeated
and Eden restored;
born as a man to die,
nailed to a cross on high,
cold in the grave to lie,
Jesus is Lord!

Source of all sovereignty,
light, immortality,
life everlasting
and heaven assured;
so with the ransomed, we
praise him eternally,
Christ in his majesty,
Jesus is Lord!

Timothy Dudley-Smith
Copyright © Timothy Dudley-Smith

307
NO EYE HAS SEEN
and no ear has heard,
and no mind has ever conceived
the glorious things
that you have prepared
for everyone who has believed;
you brought us near and you called us your own,
and made us joint heirs with your Son.

How high and how wide,
how deep and how long,
how sweet and how strong is your love;
how lavish your grace,
how faithful your ways,
how great is your love, O Lord.

Objects of mercy,
who should have known wrath,
we're filled with unspeakable joy;
riches of wisdom
unsearchable wealth,
and the wonder of knowing your voice.
You are our treasure and our great reward,
our hope and our glorious King.

Mark Altrogge. Copyright © 1990 Integrity's Hosanna! Music/
PDI Praise/Adm. by Kingsway's Thankyou Music

308
NO LONGER MINE LORD, BUT YOURS
what e'er the fight Lord, your cause,
let me have all things, let me have naught,
take every word Lord, and every thought,
I gladly yield to your command,
no longer mine, no longer mine but yours.

No longer mine Lord, but yours
to do with me as you desire.
To be exalted or laid aside,
take vain ambition and selfish pride.
Let me be humbled, you glorified,
no longer mine, no longer mine but yours.

No longer mine Lord, but yours
the sovereign Lord who we adore.
We bow before you, our glorious King,
our very lives Lord, we freely bring.
A covenant human and divine,
no longer mine, no longer mine but yours.

Geoff Baker
Copyright © 1988 Sovereign Music UK

308a The Magnificat (The song of Mary)

My soul proclaims the greatness of the Lord,
my spirit rejoices in God my Saviour;
he has looked with favour on his lowly servant.

From this day all generations will call me blessed;
the Almighty has done great things for me
and holy is his name.

He has mercy on those who fear him,
from generation to generation.

He has shown strength with his arm
and has scattered the proud in their conceit,

Casting down the mighty from their thrones
and lifting up the lowly.

He has filled the hungry with good things
and sent the rich away empty.

He has come to the aid of his servant Israel,
to remember his promise of mercy,

The promise made to our ancestors,
to Abraham and his children for ever.

Luke 1:46-55

Glory to the Father and to the Son and to the
Holy Spirit; as it was in the beginning is now
and shall be for ever. **Amen.**

From Common Worship:
Services and Prayers for the Church of England.

309

NO OTHER NAME

but the name of Jesus,
no other name but the name of the Lord;
no other name but the name of Jesus
is worthy of glory, and worthy of honour,
and worthy of power and all praise.

His name is exalted far above the earth,
his name is high above the heavens;
his name is exalted far above the earth,
give glory and honour and praise unto his name.

Robert Gay. Copyright © 1988 Integrity's Hosanna! Music/
Adm. by Kingsway's Thankyou Music

310

NO SCENES OF STATELY MAJESTY

for the King of kings;
no nights aglow with candle flame
for the King of love;
no flags of empire hung in shame for Calvary
no flowers perfumed the lonely way
that led him to a borrowed tomb for Easter Day.

No wreaths upon the ground were laid
for the King of kings;
only a crown of thorns remained
where he gave his love;
a message scrawled in irony – 'King of the Jews'
lay trampled where they turned away
and no-one knew that it was the first Easter Day.

Yet nature's finest colours blaze
for the King of kings;
and stars in jewelled clusters say
'Worship heaven's King'.
Two thousand springtimes more have bloomed,
is that enough?
O how can I be satisfied
until he hears the whole world sing of Easter love.

My prayers shall be a fragrance sweet for
the King of kings;
my love, the flowers at his feet for the King of love.
My vigil is to watch and pray until he comes;
my highest tribute to obey
and live to know the power of that first Easter Day.

I long for scenes of majesty for the risen King,
for nights aglow with candle flame
for the King of love.
A nation hushed upon its knees at Calvary:
where all our sins and griefs were nailed
and hope was born of everlasting Easter Day.

Graham Kendrick
Copyright © 1997 Ascent Music

311

NO-ONE BUT YOU, LORD

can satisfy the longing in my heart.
Nothing I do, Lord,
can take the place of drawing near to you.

Only you can fill my deepest longing,
only you can breathe in me new life;
only you can fill my heart with laughter,
only you can answer my heart's cry.

Father, I love you,
come satisfy the longing in my heart.
Fill me, overwhelm me,
until I know your love deep in my heart.

Andy Park. Copyright © 1988
Mercy/Vineyard Publishing admin by CopyCare

312

NOTHING SHALL SEPARATE US

from the love of God.
Nothing shall separate us
from the love of God.

God did not spare his only Son,
gave him to save us all.
Sin's price was met by Jesus' death
and heaven's mercy falls.

Up from the grave Jesus was raised
to sit at God's right hand;
pleading our cause in heaven's courts,
forgiven we can stand.

Now by God's grace we have embraced
a life set free from sin;
we shall deny all that destroys
our union with him.

Noel & Tricia Richards
Copyright © 1989 Kingsway's Thankyou Music

313

O FATHER OF THE FATHERLESS

in whom all families are blessed,
I love the way you father me.
You gave me life, forgave the past,
now in your arms I'm safe at last,
I love the way you father me.

Father me, forever you'll father me,
and in your embrace I'll be forever secure.
I love the way you father me.
I love the way you father me.

When bruised and broken I draw near
you hold me close and dry my tears,
I love the way you father me.

At last my fearful heart is still,
surrendered to your perfect will,
I love the way you father me.

If in my foolishness I stray,
returning empty and ashamed,
I love the way you father me.
Exchanging for my wretchedness
your radiant robes of righteousness,
I love the way you father me.

And when I look into your eyes
from deep within my spirit cries,
I love the way you father me.
Before such love I stand amazed
and ever will through endless days,
I love the way you father me.

314

O GOD MOST HIGH, ALMIGHTY KING
the champion of heaven, Lord of everything;
you've fought, you've won, death's lost its sting,
and standing in your victory we sing.

You have broken the chains
that held our captive souls.
You have broken the chains
and used them on your foes.
All your enemies are bound,
they tremble at the sound of your name;
Jesus, you have broken the chains.

The power of hell has been undone,
captivity held captive by the risen One,
and in the name of God's great Son,
we claim the mighty victory you've won.

315

O GOD OF BURNING, CLEANSING FLAME
send the fire!
Your blood-bought gift today we claim:
send the fire today!
Look down and see this waiting host,
and send the promised Holy Ghost;
we need another Pentecost!
Send the fire today! Send the fire today!

God of Elijah, hear our cry: send the fire!
and make us fit to live or die: send the fire today!
To burn up every trace of sin,
to bring the light and glory in,
the revolution now begin!
Send the fire today! Send the fire today!

It's fire we want, for fire we plead: send the fire!
The fire will meet our every need:
send the fire today!
For strength to always do what's right,
for grace to conquer in the fight,
for power to walk the world in white:
send the fire today! Send the fire today!

To make our weak hearts strong and brave:
send the fire!
To live, a dying world to save:
send the fire today!
Oh, see us on your altar lay,
we give our lives to you today,
so crown the offering now we pray:
send the fire today! Send the fire today!
Send the fire today!

316

O GIVE THANKS
to the Lord, all you his people.
O give thanks to the Lord for he is good.
Let us praise, let us thank,
let us celebrate and dance,
O give thanks to the Lord for he is good.

317

O HOLY SPIRIT, BREATHE ON ME
O Holy Spirit breathe on me,
and cleanse away my sin,
fill me with love within:
O Holy Spirit breathe on me!

O Holy Spirit fill my life,
O Holy Spirit fill my life,
take all my pride from me,
give me humility:
O Holy Spirit breathe on me!

O Holy Spirit, make me new,
O Holy Spirit, make me new,
make Jesus real to me,
give me his purity:
O Holy Spirit breathe on me!

O Holy Spirit, wind of God,
O Holy Spirit, wind of God,
give me your power today,
to live for you always:
O Holy Spirit breathe on me!

318

O HEAVEN IS IN MY HEART

O heaven is in my heart.

(Leader) The kingdom of our God is here,
(All) heaven is in my heart.
(Leader) The presence of his majesty,
(All) heaven is in my heart.
(Leader) And in his presence joy abounds,
(All) heaven is in my heart.
(Leader) The light of holiness surrounds,
(All) heaven is in my heart.

His precious life on me he spent,
heaven is in my heart.
To give me life without an end,
heaven is in my heart.
In Christ is all my confidence,
heaven is in my heart.
The hope of my inheritance,
heaven is in my heart.

We are a temple for his throne,
heaven is in my heart.
And Christ is the foundation stone,
heaven is in my heart.
He will return to take us home,
heaven is in my heart.
The Spirit and the bride say 'Come!'
Heaven is in my heart.

Graham Kendrick
Copyright © 1991 Make Way Music

319

O JESUS, I HAVE PROMISED

to serve thee to the end;
be thou forever near me,
my master and my friend.
I shall not fear the battle
if thou art by my side,
nor wander from the pathway
if thou wilt be my guide.

O let me feel thee near me;
the world is ever near;
I see the sights that dazzle,
the tempting sounds I hear;
my foes are ever near me,
around me and within;
but Jesus, draw thou nearer,
and shield my soul from sin.

O let me hear thee speaking
in accents clear and still,
above the storms of passion,
the murmurs of self-will;

O speak to reassure me,
to hasten, or control;
O speak, and make me listen,
thou guardian of my soul.

O Jesus, thou hast promised
to all who follow thee
that where thou art in glory
there shall thy servants be;
and, Jesus, I have promised
to serve thee to the end;
O give me grace to follow
my master and my friend.

O let me see thy footmarks,
and in them plant mine own;
my hope to follow duly
is in thy strength alone.
O guide me, call me, draw me,
uphold me to the end;
and then in heaven receive me,
my Saviour and my friend.

John Ernest Bode (1816-74)

320

O LET THE SON OF GOD ENFOLD YOU

with his Spirit and his love,
let him fill your heart and satisfy your soul.
O let him have the things that hold you,
and his Spirit like a dove
will descend upon your life and make you whole.

Jesus, O Jesus,
come and fill your lambs.
Jesus, O Jesus,
come and fill your lambs.

O come and sing this song with gladness
as your hearts are filled with joy,
lift your hands in sweet surrender to his name.
O give him all your tears and sadness,
give him all your years of pain,
and you'll enter into life in Jesus' name.

John Wimber
Copyright © 1979 Mercy/Vineyard Publishing admin by CopyCare

321

O LORD, HEAR MY PRAYER

O Lord, hear my prayer:
when I call answer me.

O Lord, hear my prayer,
O Lord, hear my prayer:
come and listen to me.

Jacques Berthier
Copyright © 1982, 1983 & 1984 Ateliers et Presses de Taizé

322

O LORD, I WANT TO SING YOUR PRAISES

I want to praise your name every day.
(Repeat)

Alleluia, allelu.
Alleluia, allelu.
(Alleluia.)

God, you are my God, and I will seek you;
I am satisfied when I find your love.
(Repeat)

And I will praise you as long as I live,
for your love is better than life.
(Repeat)

Alleluia...

Andy Park
Copyright © 1991 Andy Park/Kingsway's Thankyou Music

322a   I will praise you
Psalm 9:1-2

I will praise you, O Lord, with all my heart;
I will tell of all your wonders.
I will be glad and rejoice in you;
I will sing praise to your name, O Most High.

323

O LORD MY GOD!

when I in awesome wonder
consider all the works thy hand hath made,
I see the stars, I hear the mighty thunder,
thy power throughout the universe displayed:

Then sings my soul, my Saviour God to thee,
how great thou art! How great thou art!
Then sings my soul, my Saviour God to thee,
how great thou art! How great thou art!

When through the woods and forest glades I wander
and hear the birds sing sweetly in the trees;
when I look down from lofty mountain grandeur,
and hear the brook, and feel the gentle breeze;

And when I think that God his Son not sparing,
sent him to die – I scarce can take it in.
That on the cross my burden gladly bearing,
he bled and died to take away my sin:

When Christ shall come with shout of acclamation
and take me home – what joy shall fill my heart!
Then shall I bow in humble adoration
and there proclaim, my God, how great thou art!

Stuart K. Hine. Copyright © 1953 Stuart K. Hine/SK Hine Trust/
Published by Kingsway's Thankyou Music

324

O LORD OUR GOD

how majestic is your name,
the earth is filled with your glory.
O Lord our God, you are robed in majesty,
you've set your glory above the heavens.

We will magnify, we will magnify
the Lord enthroned in Zion.
We will magnify, we will magnify
the Lord enthroned in Zion.

O Lord our God,
you have established a throne,
you reign in righteousness and splendour.
O Lord our God, the skies are ringing
with your praise,
soon those on earth will come to worship.

O Lord our God, the world was made
at your command,
in you all things now hold together.
Now to him who sits on the throne
and to the Lamb,
be praise and glory and power forever.

Phil Lawson Johnston
Copyright © 1982 Kingsway's Thankyou Music

325

O LORD, OUR LORD

how majestic is your name in all the earth.
O Lord our Lord,
how majestic is your name in all the earth.
O Lord, we praise your name;
O Lord, we magnify your name.
Prince of Peace, Mighty God,
O Lord God Almighty.

Michael W. Smith. Copyright © Meadowgreen Music/
EMI Christian Music Publishing adm. by CopyCare

325a How majestic is your name
Psalm 8:1-2

O Lord, our Lord,
how majestic is your name in all the earth!

You have set your glory above the heavens.
From the lips of children and infants
you have ordained praise
because of your enemies,
to silence the foe and the avenger.

326

O LORD, THE CLOUDS ARE GATHERING

the fire of judgement burns,
how we have fallen!
O Lord, you stand appalled to see
your laws of love so scorned,
and lives so broken.

(Men)   Have mercy, Lord,
(Women) Have mercy, Lord,
(Men)   forgive us, Lord,
(Women) forgive us, Lord,
(All)   restore us, Lord,
            revive your church again.

(Men)   Let justice flow
(Women) Let justice flow
(Men)   like rivers,
(Women) like rivers,
(All)   And righteousness like a never failing stream.

O Lord, over the nations now,
where is the dove of peace?
Her wings are broken.
O Lord, while precious children starve
the tools of war increase;
their bread is stolen.

O Lord, dark powers are poised to flood
our streets with hate and fear;
we must awaken!
O Lord, let love reclaim the lives
that sin would sweep away
and let your kingdom come.

Yet, O Lord, your glorious cross shall tower
triumphant in this land,
evil confounding.
Through the fire your suffering church display
the glories of her Christ:
praises resounding!

Graham Kendrick
Copyright © 1987 Make Way Music

327

O LORD, YOUR TENDERNESS

melting all my bitterness,
O Lord, I receive your love.

O Lord, your loveliness,
changing all my ugliness,
O Lord, I receive your love.
O Lord, I receive your love,
O Lord, I receive your love.

Graham Kendrick
Copyright © 1986 Kingsway's Thankyou Music

328

O SOUL, ARE YOU WEARY AND TROUBLED?

No light in the darkness you see?
There's light for a look at the Saviour,
and life more abundant and free!

Turn your eyes upon Jesus,
look full in his wonderful face;
and the things of earth will grow strangely dim
in the light of his glory and grace.

Through death into life everlasting
he passed and we follow him there;
over us sin no more hath dominion,
for more than conquerors we are!

His word shall not fail you he promised;
believe him, and all will be well:
than go to a world that is dying,
his perfect salvation to tell.

Helen H Lemmel (1864-1961)
Copyright © 1922, 1950 Singspiration/Brentwood Benson Music

329

O THE VALLEYS SHALL RING

with the sound of praise,
and the lion shall lie with the lamb.
Of his government there shall be no end,
and his glory shall fill the earth.

May your will be done,
may your kingdom come,
let it rule, let it reign in our lives.
There's a shout in the camp as we answer the call,
hail the King, hail the Lord of lords!

Dave Bilbrough
Copyright © 1980 Kingsway's Thankyou Music

330

OH, THE MERCY OF GOD

the glory of grace,
that you chose to redeem us, to forgive and restore,
and you call us your children, chosen in him
to be holy and blameless to the glory of God.

To the praise of his glorious grace,
to the praise of his glory and power;
to him be all glory, honour and praise
forever and ever and ever, amen.

Oh, the richness of grace, the depths of his love,
in him is redemption, the forgiveness of sin.
You called us as righteous, predestined in him
for the praise of his glory, included in Christ.

Oh, the glory of God expressed in his Son,
his image and likeness revealed to us all;
the plea of the ages completed in Christ,
that we be presented perfected in him.

Geoff Bullock
Copyright © 1997 Watershed Productions/Kingsway's Thankyou Music

---

330a   The mercy of God
Hebrews 9:15

For this reason Christ is the mediator of a
new covenant, that those who are called may
receive the promised eternal inheritance now
that he has died as a ransom to set them
free from the sins committed under the first
covenant.

331
OH OUR LORD AND KING
our praise to you we bring,
there is no other rock but you.
Seated high above,
you are the one we love,
this is our song of praise to you.

King forever!
You are the first and you're the last.
You are sovereign;
all your commands will always
come to pass, to give you glory!

Who is like you?
Who else is worthy of our praise?
We exalt you;
you reign in majesty and
awesome splendour, King forever!

Abba Father,
your steadfast love will never fail.
You are faithful,
you are God and I will
worship in your courts for ever.

Alan Rose
Copyright © 1997 Kingsway's Thankyou Music

332
ONE MORE STEP
along the world I go,
one more step along the world I go.
From the old things to the new
keep me travelling along with you.

And it's from the old I travel to the new,
keep me travelling along with you.

Round the corners of the world I turn,
more and more about the world I learn.
All the new things that I see
you'll be looking at along with me.

As I travel through the bad and good,
keep me travelling the way I should.
Where I see no way to go,
you'll be telling me the way, I know.

Give me courage when the world is rough,
keep me loving though the world is tough.
Leap and sing in all I do,
keep me travelling along with you.

You are older than the world can be,
you are younger than the life in me.
Ever old and ever new,
keep me travelling along with you.

Sydney Carter
Copyright © 1971 Stainer & Bell Ltd

333
ONE SHALL TELL ANOTHER
and he shall tell his friend,
husbands, wives and children
shall come following on.
From house to house in families
shall more be gathered in,
and lights will shine in every street,
so warm and welcoming.

Come on in and taste the new wine,
the wine of the kingdom,
the wine of the kingdom of God.
Here is healing and forgiveness,
the wine of the kingdom,
the wine of the kingdom of God.

Compassion of the Father
is ready now to flow,
through acts of love and mercy
we must let it show.
He turns now from his anger
to show a smiling face,
and longs that men should stand beneath
the fountain of his grace.

He longs to do much more than
our faith has yet allowed,
to thrill us and surprise us
with his sovereign power.
Where darkness has been darkest
the brightest light will shine,
his invitation comes to us,
it's yours and it is mine.

Graham Kendrick
Copyright © 1981 Kingsway's Thankyou Music

334

ONE THING I ASK

one thing I seek,
that I may dwell in your house, O Lord.
All of my days, all of my life,
that I may see you, Lord.

Hear me, O Lord, hear me when I cry;
Lord, do not hide your face from me.
You have been my strength,
you have been my shield, and you will lift me up.

One thing I ask, one thing I desire
is to see you, is to see you.

335

ONLY BY GRACE CAN WE ENTER

only by grace can we stand;
not by our human endeavour,
but by the blood of the Lamb.
Into your presence you call us, you call us to come.
Into your presence you draw us,
and now by your grace we come,
now by your grace we come.

Lord, if you mark our transgressions,
who would stand?
Thanks to your grace we are cleansed
by the blood of the Lamb.
(Repeat)

Only by grace...

336

OPEN OUR EYES, LORD

we want to see Jesus,
to reach out and touch him
and say that we love him.
Open our ears, Lord, and help us to listen.
Open our eyes, Lord, we want to see Jesus.

337

OPEN YOUR EYES

see the glory of the King.
Lift up your voice and his praises sing.
I love you, Lord, I will proclaim:
hallelujah, I bless your name.

338

OUR CONFIDENCE IS IN THE LORD

the source of our salvation.
Rest is found in him alone,
the author of creation.
We will not fear the evil day,
because we have a refuge;
in every circumstance we say,
our hope is built on Jesus.

He is our fortress,
we will never be shaken.
He is our fortress,
we will never be shaken.
(Repeat)

We will put our trust in God.
We will put our trust in God.

339

OUR GOD IS GREAT

(Repeat x3)

He gave us the wind, the sun and the snow,
the sand on the sea shore,
the flowers that grow.
Morning and evening, winter and spring;
come join all creation and sing.

The gifts that he brings are new every day,
from glorious sunset to soft falling rain.
The mist on the hills,
the light and the shade;
come join all creation in praise.

For music and dancing,
the sounds that we hear;
for colours and words,
the life that we share, we say:

340

OUR GOD IS AN AWESOME GOD

he reigns from heaven above,
with wisdom, power and love,
our God is an awesome God!

Our God is an awesome God,
he reigns from heaven above,
with wisdom, power and love,
our God is an awesome God!

341
OVERWHELMED BY LOVE
deeper than oceans,
high as the heavens.
Ever living God, your love has rescued me.

All my sin was laid
on your dear Son, your precious one.
All my debt he paid, great is your love for me.

No-one could ever earn your love,
your grace and mercy is free.
Lord, these words are true, so is my love for you.

Noel Richards
Copyright © 1994 Kingsway's Thankyou Music

342
OVER ALL THE EARTH
you reign on high,
every mountain stream, every sunset sky.
But my one request, Lord, my only aim
is that you'd reign in me again.

Lord, reign in me, reign in your power;
over all my dreams, in my darkest hour.
You are the Lord of all I am,
so won't you reign in me again.

Over every thought, over every word,
may my life reflect the beauty of my Lord;
'cause you mean more to me
than any earthly thing.
So won't you reign in me again.

Lord, reign in me...
(Repeat)
... won't you reign in me again,
won't you reign in me again.

Brenton Brown. Copyright © 1998
Vineyard Songs (UK/Eire) admin by CopyCare

343
OVER THE MOUNTAINS AND THE SEA
your river runs with love for me,
and I will open up my heart,
and let the healer set me free.
I'm happy to be in the truth,
and I will daily lift my hands,
for I will always sing of
when your love came down, yeah.

I could sing of your love forever,
I could sing of your love forever,
I could sing of your love forever,
I could sing of your love forever.

Oh, I feel like dancing,
it's foolishness I know;
but when the world has seen the light,
they will dance with joy like we're dancing now.

Martin Smith. Copyright © 1994 Curious? Music UK/
Adm. by Kingsway's Thankyou Music

344
PEACE I GIVE TO YOU
I give to you my peace;
peace I give to you, I give to you my peace.

Let it flow to one another,
let it flow, let it flow; let it flow

Love I give to you ...

Hope I give to you ...

Joy I give to you ...

Graham Kendrick
Copyright © 1979 Kingsway's Thankyou Music

345
PEACE LIKE A RIVER
love like a mountain,
the wind of your Spirit is blowing everywhere.
Joy like a fountain, healing spring of life;
come, Holy Spirit, let your fire fall.

John Watson
Copyright © 1989 Ampelos Music admin by CopyCare

346
PEACE, PERFECT PEACE
is the gift of Christ our Lord. (Repeat)
Thus, says the Lord,
will the world know my friends.
Peace, perfect peace, is the gift of Christ our Lord.

Love, perfect love...

Faith, perfect faith...

Hope, perfect hope...

Joy, perfect joy...

Kevin Mayhew
Copyright © 1976 Kevin Mayhew Ltd

347
PEACE TO YOU
We bless you now in the name of the Lord.
Peace to you.
We bless you now in the name
of the Prince of Peace. Peace to you.

Graham Kendrick
Copyright © 1988 Make Way Music

348

PRAISE GOD FROM WHOM ALL BLESSINGS FLOW

praise him all creatures here below.
Praise him above, you heavenly host,
Praise Father, Son and Holy Ghost.
(Repeat)

Give glory to the Father,
give glory to the Son,
give glory to the Spirit
while endless ages run.

'Worthy the Lamb' all heaven cries,
'to be exalted thus:'
'Worthy the Lamb' our hearts reply,
'for he was slain for us.'

Praise God from whom all blessings flow,
Praise God from whom all blessings flow.
(Repeat x3)

Andy Piercy & Dave Clifton
Copyright © 1993 I Q Music Ltd

349

PRAISE HIM ON THE TRUMPET

the psaltery and harp,
praise him on the timbrel and the dance,
praise him with stringed instruments, too.
Praise him on the loud cymbals,
praise him on the loud cymbals,
let everything that has breath praise the Lord.

Hallelujah, praise the Lord,
hallelujah, praise the Lord,
let everything that has breath
praise the Lord.
(Repeat)

John Kennett
Copyright © 1981 Kingsway's Thankyou Music

350

PRAISE MY SOUL, THE KING OF HEAVEN

to his feet thy tribute bring.
Ransomed, healed, restored, forgiven,
who like thee his praise should sing?
Praise him! Praise him!
Praise him! Praise him!
Praise the everlasting King!

Praise him for his grace and favour
to our fathers in distress;
praise him, still the same forever,
slow to chide, and swift to bless.

Praise him! Praise him!
Praise him! Praise him!
Glorious in his faithfulness.

Father-like, he tends and spares us;
well our feeble frame he knows;
in his hands he gently bears us,
rescues us from all our foes.
Praise him! Praise him!
Praise him! Praise him!
Widely as his mercy flows.

Angels help us to adore him;
ye behold him face to face;
Sun and moon, bow down before him,
dwellers all in time and space.
Praise him! Praise him!
Praise him! Praise him!
Praise with us the God of grace!

Henry Francis Lyte (1793-1847)

350a   Kyrie confession

Leader   God be gracious to us and bless us,
and make your face shine upon us;
Lord, have mercy.

All   **Lord, have mercy.**

Leader   May your ways be known on
the earth,
your saving power among the nations;
Christ, have mercy.

All   **Christ, have mercy.**

Leader   You, Lord, have made known your
salvation, and reveal your justice
in the sight of the nations:
Lord, have mercy.

All   **Lord, have mercy.**

Absolution

The Lord enrich *you* with his grace,
and nourish *you* with his blessing;
the Lord defend *you* in trouble
and keep *you* from all evil;
the Lord accept *your* prayers,
and absolve *you* from *your* offences,
for the sake of Jesus Christ, our Saviour.
Amen.

From Common Worship:
Services and Prayers for the Church of England.

351
PRAISE THE LORD

all you servants of the Lord,
who minister by night within his house.
Lift up your hands within the sanctuary,
and praise the Lord.

May the Lord, the maker of heaven and earth,
may this Lord bless you from Zion;
lift up your hands within the sanctuary
and praise the Lord.

We praise you, Lord, we praise you, Lord:
hallelujah, we praise you, Lord.

Ian White. Copyright © 1985
Little Misty Music/Kingsway's Thankyou Music

352
PRAISE THE NAME OF JESUS

praise the name of Jesus,
he's my rock, he's my fortress,
he's my deliverer, in him will I trust.
Praise the name of Jesus.

Roy Hicks Jnr. Copyright © 1975 Latter Rain Music/
EMI Christian Music Publishing admin by CopyCare

353
PRAISE YOU, LORD

for the wonder of your healing.
Praise you, Lord, for your love so freely given;
outpouring, anointing,
flowing in to heal our wounds:
praise you, Lord, for your love for me.

Praise you, Lord, for your gift of liberation.
Praise you, Lord, you have set the captives free;
the chains that bind are broken
by the sharpness of your sword:
Praise you, Lord, you gave your life for me.

Praise you, Lord,
you have borne the depths of sorrow.
Praise you, Lord, for your anguish on the tree;
the nails that tore your body
and the pain that tore your soul:
praise you, Lord, your tears they fell for me.

Praise you, Lord,
you have turned our thorns to roses.
Glory, Lord, as they bloom upon your brow;
the path of pain is hallowed,
for your love has made it sweet;
praise you, Lord, and may I love you now.

Nettie Rose
Copyright © 1977 Kingsway's Thankyou Music

354
PURIFY MY HEART

let me be as gold
and precious silver.
Purify my heart,
let me be as gold,
pure gold.

Refiner's fire,
my heart's one desire
is to be holy,
set apart for you, Lord.
I choose to be holy,
set apart for you, my master,
ready to do your will.

Purify my heart,
cleanse me from within
and make me holy.
Purify my heart,
cleanse me from my sin,
deep within.

Brian Doerksen. Copyright © 1990
Mercy/Vineyard Publishing admin by CopyCare

354a   The goal of faith
1 Peter 1:8-9

Though you have not seen him, you love
him; and even though you do not see
him now, you believe in him and are
filled with an inexpressible and glorious joy,
for you are receiving the goal of your faith,
the salvation of your souls.

355
QUIET MY MIND LORD

make me still before you;
calm my restless heart, Lord,
make me more like you.

Quiet my mind Lord
make me still before you;
calm my restless heart, Lord,
make me more like you.

Raise up my hands that are hanging down;
strengthen my feeble knees.
May your love and joy abound,
and fill me with your peace.

Tracy Orrison. Copyright © 1990
Sound Truth Publishing/Kingsway's Thankyou Music

356
RECONCILED, I'M RECONCILED,
I'm reconciled to God for ever;
know he took away my sin,
I know his love will leave me never.
Reconciled, I am his child,
I know it was on me he smiled,
I'm reconciled, I'm reconciled to God.

Hallelujah, I'm justified, I'm justified,
it's just as if I'd never sinned,
and once I knew such guilty fear,
but now I know his peace within me.
Justified, I'm justified,
it's all because my Jesus died,
I'm justified, I'm justified by God.

Hallelujah I'll magnify, I'll magnify,
I'll magnify his name for ever,
wear the robe of righteousness
and bless the name of Jesus, Saviour.
Magnify the one who died,
the one who reigns for me on high,
I'll magnify, I'll magnify my God.

Mike Kerry
Copyright © 1984 Kingsway's Thankyou Music

357
REJOICE! REJOICE!
Christ is in you,
the hope of glory in our hearts.
He lives! He lives! His breath is in you,
arise a mighty army, we arise.

Now is the time for us
to march upon the land,
into our hands he will give the ground we claim.
He rides in majesty
to lead us into victory,
the world shall see that Christ is Lord!

God is at work in us
his purpose to perform,
building a kingdom of power not of words,
where things impossible,
by faith shall be made possible;
let's give the glory to him now.

Though we are weak, his grace
is everything we need;
we're made of clay but this treasure is within.
He turns our weaknesses
into his opportunities,
so that the glory goes to him.

Graham Kendrick
Copyright © 1983 Kingsway's Thankyou Music

358
REIGN IN ME
Sovereign Lord, reign in me.
Reign in me,
Sovereign Lord, reign in me.

Captivate my heart,
let your kingdom come,
establish there your throne,
let your will be done.

Chris Bowater
Copyright © 1985 Sovereign Lifestyle Music

359
RESTORE, O LORD
the honour of your name,
in works of sovereign power
come shake the earth again;
that men may see
and come with reverent fear
to the living God,
whose kingdom shall outlast the years.

Restore, O Lord,
in all the earth your fame,
and in our time revive
the church that bears your name.
And in your anger,
Lord, remember mercy,
O living God,
whose mercy shall outlast the years.

Bend us, O Lord,
where we are hard and cold,
in your refiner's fire
come purify the gold.
Though suffering comes
and evil crouches near,
still our living God
is reigning, he is reigning here.

(Repeat verse 1)

Graham Kendrick & Chris Rolinson
Copyright © 1981 Kingsway's Thankyou Music

360
RIVER, WASH OVER ME
cleanse me and make me new.
Bathe me, refresh me and fill me anew,
river wash over me.

Spirit, watch over me,
lead me to Jesus' feet.
Cause me to worship and fill me anew,
Spirit, watch over me.

Jesus, rule over me,
reign over all my heart.
Teach me to praise you and fill me anew,
Jesus, rule over me.

361
SAFE IN THE SHADOW OF THE LORD

beneath his hand and power,
I trust in him, I trust in him,
my fortress and my tower.

My hope is set on God alone,
though Satan spreads his snare,
I trust in him, I trust in him
to keep me in his care.

From fears and phantoms of the night,
from foes about my way,
I trust in him, I trust in him
by darkness as by day.

His holy angels keep my feet
secure from every stone;
I trust in him, I trust in him
and unafraid go on.

Strong in the everlasting name,
and in my Father's care,
I trust in him, I trust in him
who hears and answers prayer.

Safe in the shadow of the Lord,
possessed by love divine,
I trust in him, I trust in him
and meet his love with mine.

362
SALVATION BELONGS TO OUR GOD

who sits on the throne,
and to the Lamb.
Praise and glory, wisdom and thanks,
honour and power and strength:

Be to our God forever and ever,
be to our God forever and ever,
be to our God forever and ever, amen.

And we, the redeemed shall be strong
in purpose and unity,
declaring aloud,
praise and glory, wisdom and thanks,
honour and power and strength:

362a   Prayer of humble access

Most merciful Lord,
your love compels us to come in.
Our hands were unclean,
our hearts were unprepared;
we were not fit even to eat the crumbs
    from under your table.
But you, Lord, are the God of our salvation,
and share your bread with sinners.
So cleanse and feed us with the precious
body and blood of your Son,
that he may live in us and we in him;
and that we, with the whole company of
Christ, may sit and eat in your kingdom.
Amen.

363
SAY THE WORD

I will be healed;
you are the great physician,
you meet every need.
Say the word, I will be free;
where chains have held me captive,
come sing your songs to me, say the word.

Say the word, I will be filled;
my hands reach out to heaven,
where striving is stilled.
Say the word, I will be changed;
where I am dry and thirsty,
send cool, refreshing rain, say the word.

His tears have fallen like rain on my life;
each drop a fresh revelation.
I will return to the place of the cross,
where grace and mercy
pour from heaven's throne.

Say the word, I will be poor,
that I might know the riches
that you have in store.
Say the word, I will be weak;
your strength will be the power
that satisfies the meek. Say the word.

The Lord will see the travail of his soul,
and he and I will be satisfied.
Complete the work you have started in me:
O, come Lord Jesus, shake my life again.

Say the word, say the word.

364

SEARCH ME, O GOD

and know my heart;
know all my thoughts and my ways.
Cleanse me, O God,
give me a pure heart,
that I may see your face.

For you are an all consuming fire!
For you are an all consuming fire!

Teach me, O God, show me your ways,
and I will walk in your truth.
Keep me, O God, keep me from falling,
that I may stand before you.

Fill me, O God, and send me out,
and I will make you known.
Give me your heart and your compassion,
and let your mercy flow.

Paul Oakley
Copyright © 1997 Kingsway's Thankyou Music

364a   Search me, O God
Psalm 139:23-24

Search me, O God, and know my heart;
test me and know my anxious thoughts.
See if there is any offensive way in me,
and lead me in the way everlasting.

365

SEEK YE FIRST

the kingdom of God
and his righteousness,
and all these things shall be added unto you,
hallelu, hallelujah!

Hallelujah! Hallelujah!
Hallelujah! Hallelu, hallelujah!

Man shall not live by bread alone,
but by every word
that proceeds from the mouth of God,
hallelu, hallelujah!

Ask and it shall be given unto you,
seek and ye shall find.
Knock and it shall be opened unto you,
hallelu, hallelujah!

If the Son shall set you free,
ye shall be free indeed.
Ye shall know the truth and the truth shall set you
free, hallelu, hallelujah!

Let your light so shine before men
that they may see your good works
and glorify your Father in heaven,
hallelu, hallelujah!

Trust in the Lord with all thine heart,
he shall direct thy paths,
in all thy ways acknowledge him,
hallelu, hallelujah!

Karen Lafferty
Copyright © 1972 Maranatha! Music admin. by CopyCare

366

SEND ME OUT FROM HERE LORD

to serve a world in need.
May I know no man by the coat he wears,
but the heart that Jesus sees.
And may the light of your face
shine upon me, Lord.
You have filled my heart
with the greatest joy,
and my cup is overflowing.

'Go now, and carry the news
to all creation,
every race and tongue.
Take no purse with you,
take nothing to eat
for he will supply your needs.'

'Go now, bearing the light,
living for others,
fearlessly walking into the night;
take no thought for your lives,
like lambs among wolves,
full of the Spirit, ready to die.'

John Pantry
Copyright © Harper Collins Religious/Adm. by CopyCare

366a   The great commission
Matthew 28:18-20

Then Jesus came to them and said,
'All authority in heaven and on earth
   has been given to me.
Therefore go and make disciples
   of all nations,
baptising them in the name of the Father
and of the Son and of the Holy Spirit,
and teaching them to obey everything
   I have commanded you.
And surely I am with you always,
to the very end of the age.'

367
SHOUT FOR JOY AND SING,
LET YOUR PRAISES RING
see that God is building
a kingdom for a King.
His dwelling place with men, the new Jerusalem;
where Jesus is Lord over all.

And we will worship, worship,
we will worship Jesus the Lord.
(Repeat)

A work so long concealed,
in time will be revealed,
as the sons of God shall rise and take their stand.
Clothed in his righteousness,
the church made manifest,
where Jesus is Lord over all.

Sovereign over all, hail him risen Lord.
He alone is worthy of our praise.
Reigning in majesty, ruling in victory,
Jesus is Lord over all.

Dave Bilbrough
Copyright © 1983 Kingsway's Thankyou Music

368
SHOUT FOR JOY AND SING
YOUR PRAISES TO THE KING
lift your voice and let your hallelujahs ring;
come before his throne to worship and adore,
enter joyfully now the presence of the Lord.
You are my Creator,
you are my Deliverer,
you are my Redeemer, you are Lord,
and you are my Healer.
You are my Provider,
you are now my Shepherd and my guide,
Jesus, Lord and King, I worship you.

David Fellingham
Copyright © 1988 Kingsway's Thankyou Music

369
SHOW ME THE WAY OF THE CROSS
once again, denying myself for the love that I've gained.
Everything's you now, everything's changed;
it's time you had my whole life, you can have it all.

Yes, I resolve to give it all;
some things must die, some things must live,
not 'what can I gain'? But 'what can I give?'
If much is required when much is received,
then you can have my whole life,
Jesus, have it all.

I've given like a beggar but lived like the rich,
and crafted myself a more comfortable cross.
Yet what I am called to is deeper than this;
it's time you had my whole life,
you can have it all.

Matt Redman
Copyright © 1996 Kingsway's Thankyou Music

370
SHOW YOUR POWER, O LORD
demonstrate the justice of your kingdom.
Prove your mighty word,
vindicate your name before a watching world.
Awesome are your deeds, O Lord;
renew them for this hour.
Show your power, O Lord,
among the people now.

Show your power, O Lord,
cause your church to rise and take action.
Let all fear be gone,
powers of the age to come are breaking through.
We your people are ready to serve,
to arise and to obey.
Show your power, O Lord,
and set the people free.

Graham Kendrick
Copyright © 1988 Make Way Music

371
SING A SONG OF CELEBRATION
lift up a shout of praise,
for the Bridegroom will come, the glorious One.
And oh, we will look on his face;
we'll go to a much better place.

Dance with all your might,
lift up your hands and clap for joy:
the time's drawing near when he will appear.
And oh, we will stand by his side;
a strong, pure, spotless bride.

(oh) We will dance on the streets that are golden,
the glorious bride and the great Son of Man,
from every tongue and tribe and nation
will join in the song of the Lamb.

(Men-Women echo)
Sing aloud for the time of rejoicing is near.
The risen King, our Groom is soon to appear.
The wedding feast to come is now near at hand.
Lift up your voice, proclaim the coming Lamb.

We will dance...

David Ruis. Copyright © 1993
Mercy/Vineyard Publishing/Adm. by CopyCare

372

SING TO GOD
NEW SONGS OF WORSHIP

all his deeds are marvellous;
he has brought salvation to us
with his hand and holy arm:
he has shown to all the nations
righteousness and saving power;
he recalled his truth and mercy
to his people Israel.

Sing to God new songs of worship:
earth has seen his victory;
let the lands of earth be joyful
praising him with thankfulness:
sound upon the harp his praises,
play to him with melody;
let the trumpets sound his triumph,
show your joy to God the King!

Sing to God new songs of worship:
let the sea now make a noise;
all on earth and in the waters
sound your praises to the Lord:
let the hills be joyful together,
let the rivers clap their hands,
for with righteousness and justice
he will come to judge the earth.

Michael Baughen
Words copyright © Michael Baughen/Jubilate Hymns

373

SING TO THE LORD

with all of your heart;
sing of the glory that's due to his name.
Sing to the Lord with all of your soul,
join all of heaven and earth to proclaim:

You are the Lord,
the Saviour of all,
God of creation, we praise you.
We sing the songs
that awaken the dawn,
God of creation, we praise you.

Sing to the Lord
with all of your mind,
with understanding
give thanks to the King.
Sing to the Lord
with all of your strength,
living our lives as a praise offering.

Stuart Garrard
Copyright © 1994 Kingsway's Thankyou Music

373a A prayer for guidance
of the Holy Spirit

God, who from of old
taught the hearts of your faithful people
by sending to them
the light of your Holy Spirit:
grant us by the same Spirit
to have a right judgement in all things
and evermore to rejoice in his holy comfort;
through the merits of
Christ Jesus our Saviour.
Amen.

From Common Worship:
Services and Prayers for the Church of England.

374

SO FREELY

flows the endless love you give to me;
so freely, not dependent on my part.
As I am reaching out
reveal the love within your heart,
as I am reaching out
reveal the love within your heart.

Completely, that's the way
you give your love to me;
completely, not dependent on my part.
As I am reaching out
reveal the love within your heart,
as I am reaching out
reveal the love within your heart.

So easy, I receive
the love you give to me;
so easy, not dependent on my part.
Flowing out to me
the love within your heart,
flowing out to me
the love within your heart.

Dave Bilbrough
Copyright © 1983 Kingsway's Thankyou Music

374a   This is love
1 John 4:10

This is love:
not that we loved God,
but that he loved us and sent his Son
as an atoning sacrifice for our sins.

375

SOON, AND VERY SOON

we are going to see the King.
Soon, and very soon,
we are going to see the King.
Soon, and very soon,
we are going to see the King.
Alleluia, alleluia,
we're going to see the King!

No more crying there
we are going to see the King...

No more dying there
we are going to see the King...

Alleluia, alleluia,
Alleluia, alleluia.

Soon, and very soon,
we are going to see the King...

Alleluia ...

Andrae Crouch. Copyright © 1976 Bud John Songs/Crouch Music Co/
EMI Christian Music Publishing/ Adm. by CopyCare

376

SOUND THE TRUMPET

strike the drum,
see the King of glory come,
join the praises rising from
the people of the Lord.
Let your voices now be heard,
unrestrained and unreserved,
prepare the way for his return,
you people of the Lord.

Sing Jesus is Lord; Jesus is Lord.
Bow down to his authority,
for he has slain the enemy.
Of heaven and hell he holds the key.
Jesus is Lord; Jesus is Lord.

Dave Bilbrough
Copyright © 1991 Kingsway's Thankyou Music

377

SOFTEN MY HEART LORD,

soften my heart.
From all indifference
set me apart,
to feel your compassion,
to weep with your tears;
come soften my heart, O Lord,
soften my heart.

Graham Kendrick
Copyright © 1988 Make Way Music

378

SPIRIT OF GOD

show me Jesus,
remove the darkness,
let truth shine through!
Spirit of God, show me Jesus,
reveal the fulness of his love to me.

Chris Bowater
Copyright © 1978 Sovereign Lifestyle Music

379

SPIRIT OF THE LIVING GOD

fall afresh on me;
Spirit of the living God,
fall afresh on me.
Fill me anew, fill me anew.
Spirit of the Lord
fall afresh on me.

Paul Armstong. Copyright © 1984 Restoration Music
admin. by Sovereign Music UK

380

SPIRIT OF THE LIVING GOD

fall afresh on me;
Spirit of the living God,
fall afresh on me.
Break me, melt me, mould me, fill me.
Spirit of the living God,
fall afresh on me.

Daniel Iverson. Copyright © 1935 Birdwing Music/
EMI Christian Music Publishing/Adm. by CopyCare

381

STANDING IN YOUR PRESENCE

Lord, my heart and life are changed;
just to love you and to live to
see your beauty and your grace.

Heaven and earth cry out your name,
nations rise up and see your face;
and your kingdom is established
as I live to know you more.
Now I will never be the same;
Spirit of God, my life you've changed,
and I'll forever sing your praise.
I live to know you, Lord.
I live to know you, Lord.

You've called me, I will follow;
your will for me I'm sure.
Let your heartbeat be my heart's cry,
let me live to serve your call.

Darlene Zschech. Copyright © 1996 Darlene Zschech/
Hillsong Publishing/Kingsway's Thankyou Music

382

SUCH LOVE, PURE AS THE WHITEST SNOW

such love, weeps for the shame I know;
such love, paying the debt I owe;
O Jesus, such love.

Such love, stilling my restlessness;
such love, filling my emptiness;
such love, showing me holiness;
O Jesus, such love.

Such love, springs from eternity;
such love, streaming through history;
such love, fountain of life to me;
O Jesus, such love.

Graham Kendrick
Copyright © 1988 Make Way Music

382a   Te Deum Laudamus

We praise you, O God,
we acclaim you as the Lord;
all creation worships you,
the Father everlasting.
To you all angels, all the powers of heaven,
the cherubim and seraphim,
    sing in endless praise:
Holy, holy, holy Lord,
    God of power and might,
heaven and earth are full of your glory.
The glorious company of apostles praise you.
The noble fellowship of prophets praise you.
The white-robed army of martyrs praise you.
Throughout the world the holy Church
    acclaims you:
Father, of majesty unbounded,
your true and only Son, worthy of all praise,
the Holy Spirit, advocate and guide.

You, Christ, are the King of glory,
the eternal Son of the Father.
When you took our flesh to set us free
you humbly chose the Virgin's womb.
You overcame the sting of death
and opened the kingdom of heaven
    to all believers.
You are seated at God's right hand in glory.
We believe that you will come
    and be our judge.
Come then, Lord, and help your people,
bought with the price of your own blood,
and bring us with your saints
to glory everlasting.

From Common Worship:
Services and Prayers for the Church of England.

383

SUCH LOVE, SUCH GRACE

makes the pieces come falling into place,
breaks through the darkness, turns on the light,
making blindness give way to sight.

Your love has conquered, has set us free
to become all you've called us to be,
healing the wounded, making us stand,
bringing peace and a sword in our hand.

And no power in the universe
can separate us from the love of God.
We're yours forever with nothing to fear,
willing slaves to the love that brought us here.

Dave Bryant
Copyright © 1982 Kingsway's Thankyou Music

384

SURELY OUR GOD

is the God of gods,
and the Lord of kings,
the revealer of mysteries.
Surely our God is the God of gods,
and the Lord of kings,
the revealer of mysteries.

He changes the times and the seasons,
he gives rhythm to the tides,
he knows what is hidden
in the darkest of places,
brings the shadows into his light.

I'll praise you always my Father,
you are Lord of heaven and earth.
You hide your secret
from the 'wise' and the learned,
and reveal them to this, your child.

Thank you for sending your only Son,
we may know the mystery of God;
he opens the treasures
of wisdom and knowledge
to the humble, not to the proud.

David & Liz Morris
Copyright © 1996 Kingsway's Thankyou Music

385

TAKE US TO THE RIVER

take us there in unity to sing
a song of your salvation
to win this generation for our King.
A song of your forgiveness
for it is with grace that river flows;
take us to the river in the city of our God.

Take us to your throne room
give us ears to hear the cry of heaven;
for that cry is mercy
mercy to the fallen sons of man
for mercy has triumphed;
triumphed over judgement by your blood
take us to the throne room
in the city of our God.

For the Spirit of the Sovereign Lord is upon us;
this is the year of the Lord.
For the Spirit of the Sovereign Lord is upon us;
this is the year of the Lord.

Take us to the mountain,
lift us in the shadow of your hands;
is this your mighty angel,
who stands astride the ocean and the land?
For in his hand your mercy
showers on a dry and barren place;
take us to the mountain
in the city of our God.

For the Spirit of the Sovereign Lord is upon us;
this is the year of the Lord.
For the Spirit of the Sovereign Lord is upon us;
this is the year of the Lord.

386
TEACH ME TO DANCE
to the beat of your heart,
teach me to move in the power of your Spirit,
teach me to walk in the light of your presence,
teach me to dance to the beat of your heart.

Teach me to love with your heart of compassion,
teach me to trust in the word of your promise,
teach me to hope in the day of your coming,
teach me to dance to the beat of your heart.

You wrote the rhythm of life,
created heaven and earth;
in you is joy without measure.
So, like a child in your sight,
I dance to see your delight,
for I was made for your pleasure, pleasure.

Let all my movements express
a heart that loves to say 'yes',
a will that leaps to obey you.
Let all my energy blaze to see the joy in your face;
let my whole being praise you, praise you.

387
TELL OUT, MY SOUL
the greatness of the Lord!
Unnumbered blessings, give my spirit voice;
tender to me the promise of his word;
in God my Saviour shall my heart rejoice.

Tell out, my soul, the greatness of his name!
Make known his might, the deeds his arm has done;
his mercy sure, from age to age the same;
his holy name – the Lord, the mighty One.

Tell out, my soul, the greatness of his might!
Powers and dominions lay their glory by;
proud hearts and stubborn wills are put to flight,
the hungry fed, the humble lifted high.

Tell out, my soul, the glories of his word!
Firm is his promise, and his mercy sure.
Tell out, my soul, the greatness of the Lord
to children's children and forever more!

388
THANK YOU LORD, FOR THIS FINE DAY
(Repeat x2)
right where we are.

Alleluia, praise the Lord! (Repeat x2)
Right where we are.

Thank you, Lord, for loving us...

Thank you, Lord, for giving us peace...

Thank you, Lord, for setting us free...

389
THANK YOU FOR SAVING ME
what can I say?
You are my everything, I will sing your praise.
You shed your blood for me; what can I say?
You took my sin and shame, a sinner called by name.

Great is the Lord. Great is the Lord.
For we know your truth has set us free;
you've set your hope in me.

Mercy and grace are mine, forgiven is my sin;
Jesus, my only hope, the Saviour of the world.
'Great is the Lord,' we cry;
God, let your kingdom come.
Your word has let me see, thank you for saving me.

390

THANK YOU FOR THE CROSS

the price you paid for us,
how you gave yourself, so completely,
precious Lord (precious Lord).
Now our sins are gone, all forgiven,
covered by your blood, all forgotten,
thank you, Lord (thank you, Lord).

Oh, I love you, Lord,
really love you, Lord.
I will never understand why you love me.
You're my deepest joy,
you're my heart's desire,
and the greatest thing of all,
O Lord, I see: you delight in me!

For our healing there, Lord, you suffered,
and to take our fear you poured out your love,
precious Lord (precious Lord).
Calvary's work is done, you have conquered,
able now to save so completely,
thank you, Lord (thank you, Lord).

Graham Kendrick
Copyright © 1985 Kingsway's Thankyou Music

391

THANK YOU, JESUS

thank you, Jesus,
thank you, Lord, for loving me.
Thank you, Jesus, thank you, Jesus,
thank you, Lord, for loving me.

You went to Calvary,
and there you died for me,
thank you, Lord, for loving me.
You went to Calvary,
and there you died for me,
thank you, Lord, for loving me.

You rose up from the grave,
to me new life you gave,
thank you, Lord, for loving me.
You rose up from the grave,
to me new life you gave,
thank you, Lord, for loving me.

You're coming back again,
and we with you shall reign,
thank you, Lord, for loving me.
You're coming back again,
and we with you shall reign,
thank you, Lord, for loving me.

Alison Huntley
Copyright © 1978 Kingsway's Thankyou Music

391a The sacrifice of Christ
John 3:16-17

For God so loved the world that he gave his
one and only Son, that whoever believes in
him shall not perish but have eternal life.
For God did not send his Son into the world
to condemn the world, but to save the world
through him.

392

THANK YOU,
THANK YOU FOR THE BLOOD

that you shed, standing in its blessing,
we sing these freedom songs.

Thank you, thank you
for the battle you won,
standing in your victory
we sing salvation songs
we sing salvation songs.

You have opened a way to the Father,
where before we could never have come.
Jesus, count us as yours now forever,
as we sing these freedom songs.
(Repeat)

We sing of all you've done
we sing of all you've done
we sing of all you've done for us,
won for us, paid for us.
(Repeat)

Matt Redman
Copyright © 1999 Kingsway's Thankyou Music

393

THE CHURCH'S ONE FOUNDATION

is Jesus Christ, her Lord;
she is his new creation
by water and the word;
from heaven he came and sought her
to be his holy bride,
with his own blood he bought her,
and for her life he died.

Elect from every nation,
yet one o'er all the earth,
her charter of salvation –
one Lord, one faith, one birth;
one holy name she blesses,
partakes one holy food,
and to one hope she presses
with every grace endued.

Though with a scornful wonder
men see her sore oppressed,
by schisms rent asunder,
by heresies distressed,
yet saints their watch are keeping,
their cry goes up, 'How long?'
And soon the night of weeping
shall be the morn of song.

'Mid toil, and tribulation,
and tumult of her war,
she waits the consummation
of peace forever more;
till with the vision glorious
her longing eyes are blessed,
and the great church victorious
shall be the church at rest.

Yet she on earth hath union
with God the Three in One,
and mystic sweet communion
with those whose rest is won:
O happy ones and holy!
Lord, give us grace that we,
like them, the meek and lowly,
on high may dwell with thee.

Words: Samuel John Stone

394
THE CROSS HAS SAID IT ALL
the cross has said it all.
I can't deny what you have shown,
the cross speaks of a God of love;
there displayed for all to see,
Jesus Christ, our only hope,
a message of the Father's heart:
'Come, my children, come on home.'

As high as the heavens are above the earth,
so high is the measure of your great love;
as far as the east is from the west,
so far have you taken our sins from us.
(Repeat)

The cross has said it all,
the cross has said it all.
I never recognised your touch
until I met you at the cross;
we are fallen, dust to dust,
how could you do this for us?
Son of God shed precious blood:
who can comprehend this love?

How high, how wide, how deep; (x4)
how high!

Matt Redman & Martin Smith
Copyright © 1995 Kingsway's Thankyou Music

394a   The love of Christ
Ephesians 3:17b-19

And I pray that you, being rooted and
established in love, may have power, together
with all the saints, to grasp how wide and
long and high and deep is the love of
Christ, and to know this love that surpasses
knowledge that you may be filled to the
measure of all the fullness of God.

395
THE CRUCIBLE FOR SILVER
and the furnace for gold,
but the Lord tests the heart of this child.
Standing in all purity,
God, our passion is for holiness,
lead us to the secret place of praise.

Jesus, holy One,
you are my heart's desire.
King of kings, my everything,
you've set this heart on fire.
(Repeat)

Father, take our offering,
with our song we humbly praise you.
You have brought your holy fire to our lips.
Standing in your beauty, Lord,
your gift to us is holiness;
lead us to the place where we can sing:

Martin Smith
Copyright © 1993 Kingsway's Thankyou Music

396
THE EARTH IS THE LORD'S
(Women) and everything in it,
(Men)   the earth is the Lord's,
(Women) the work of his hands.
(Men)   The earth is the Lord's
(Women) and everything in it;
(All)   and all things were made
                for his glory.

(Last time)
(All)   and all things were made,
                yes, all things were made,
                and all things were made for his glory.

The mountains are his, the seas and the islands,
the cities and towns, the houses and streets.
Let rebels bow down and worship before him,
for all things were made for his glory.

Graham Kendrick
Copyright © 1986 Kingsway's Thankyou Music

397
THE KING OF LOVE IS MY DELIGHT

his eyes are fire, his face is light,
the First and Last, the Living One,
his name is Jesus.
And from his mouth there comes a sound
that shakes the earth and splits the ground,
and yet this voice is life to me,
the voice of Jesus.

And I will sing my songs of love,
calling out across the earth;
the King has come, the King of love has come.
And troubled minds can know his peace,
captive hearts can be released;
the King has come, the King of love has come.

My Lover's breath is sweetest wine,
I am his prize, and he is mine;
how can a sinner know such joy?
Because of Jesus.
The wounds of love are in his hands,
the price is paid for sinful man;
accepted child, forgiven son, because of Jesus.

And my desire is to have you near;
Lord, you know that you are welcome here.
Before such love, before such grace
I will let the walls come down.

Stuart Townend & Kevin Jamieson
Copyright © 1997 Kingsway's Thankyou Music

398
THE KING OF LOVE MY SHEPHERD IS

whose goodness faileth never.
I nothing lack if I am his
and he is mine forever.

Where streams of living water flow
my ransomed soul he leadeth.
And where the verdant pastures grow
with food celestial feedeth.

Perverse and foolish oft I strayed
but yet in love he sought me.
And on his shoulder gently laid,
and home rejoicing brought me.

In death's dark vale I fear no ill,
with thee, dear Lord, beside me.
Thy rod and staff my comfort still,
thy cross before to guide me.

Thou spread'st a table in my sight;
thy unction grace bestoweth.
And O what transport of delight
from thy pure chalice floweth!

And so through all the length of days
thy goodness faileth never.
Good Shepherd, may I sing thy praise
within thy house forever.

H. W. Baker (1821-77)

399
THE KING OF LOVE MY SHEPHERD IS

whose goodness faileth never.
I nothing lack if I am his
and he is mine forever.

Where streams of living water flow
my ransomed soul he leadeth.
And where the verdant pastures grow
with food celestial feedeth.

Perverse and foolish oft I strayed
but yet in love he sought me.
And on his shoulder gently laid,
and home rejoicing brought me.

In death's dark vale I fear no ill,
with thee, dear Lord, beside me.
Thy rod and staff my comfort still,
thy cross before to guide me.

Thou spread'st a table in my sight;
thy unction grace bestoweth.
And O what transport of delight
from thy pure chalice floweth!

And so through all the length of days
thy goodness faileth never.
Good Shepherd, may I sing thy praise
within thy house forever.

H. W. Baker (1821-77)

400
THE KING IS AMONG US

his Spirit is here,
let's draw near and worship,
let songs fill the air.

He looks down upon us,
delight in his face,
enjoying his children's love,
enthralled by our praise.

For each child is special,
accepted and loved,
a love gift from Jesus
to his Father above.

And now he is giving
his gifts to us all,
for no one is worthless
and each one is called.

The Spirit's anointing
on all flesh comes down,
and we shall be channels
for works like his own.

We come now believing
your promise of power,
for we are your people
and this is your hour.

The King is among us,
his Spirit is here,
let's draw near and worship,
let songs fill the air.

Graham Kendrick
Copyright © 1981 Kingsway's Thankyou Music

401
THE LORD HAS LED FORTH
his people with joy,
and his chosen ones with singing, singing.
The Lord has led forth his people with joy,
and his chosen ones with singing.

He has giv'n to them
the lands of the nations,
to possess the fruit and keep his laws,
and praise, praise his name.

Chris Bowater
Copyright © 1982 Sovereign Lifestyle Music

402
THE LIGHT OF CHRIST
has come into the world;
the light of Christ
has come into the world.

All men must be born again
to see the kingdom of God;
the water and the Spirit
bring new life in God's love.

God gave up his only Son
out of love for the world,
so that all men who believe in him
will live forever.

The light of God has come to us
so that we might have salvation;
from the darkness of our sins we walk
into glory with Christ Jesus.

Donald Fishel
Copyright © 1974 The Word of God Music adm. by CopyCare

403
THE LORD IS MARCHING OUT
in splendour,
in awesome majesty he rides,
for truth, humility and justice,
his mighty army fills the skies.

O give thanks to the Lord for his love endures,
O give thanks to the Lord for his love endures,
O give thanks to the Lord for his love endures,
for ever, for ever.

His army marches out with dancing
for he has filled our hearts with joy.
Be glad the kingdom is advancing,
the love of God our battle cry!

Graham Kendrick
Copyright © 1986 Kingsway's Thankyou Music

403a   I will praise you, O Lord
Psalm 108:3-5

I will praise you, O Lord, among the nations;
I will sing of you among the peoples.
For great is your love, higher than the
heavens; your faithfulness reaches to the skies.
Be exalted, O God, above the heavens,
and let your glory be over all the earth.

404
THE LORD REIGNS
the Lord reigns,
the Lord reigns,
let the earth rejoice, let the earth rejoice,
let the earth rejoice.
Let the people be glad
that our God reigns.
(Repeat)

A fire goes before him
and burns up all his enemies;
the hills melt like wax
at the presence of the Lord,
at the presence of the Lord.

The heavens declare his righteousness,
the peoples see his glory;
for you, O Lord, are exalted
over all the earth,
over all the earth.

Daniel Stradwick. Copyright © 1980 Scripture in Song
a division of Integrity Music/Adm. by Kingsway's Thankyou Music

405
THE LORD'S MY SHEPHERD

I'll not want;
he makes me down to lie in pastures green;
he leadeth me the quiet waters by.

My soul he doth restore again;
and me to walk doth make
within the paths of righteousness,
e'en for his own name's sake.

Yea, though I walk in death's dark vale,
yet will I fear no ill;
for thou art with me; and thy rod
and staff me comfort still.

My table thou hast furnishèd
in presence of my foes;
my head thou dost with oil anoint,
and my cup overflows.

Goodness and mercy all my life
shall surely follow me;
and in God's house forever more
my dwelling place shall be.

Psalm 23. Words: Scottish Psalter (1650)

406
THE LORD'S MY SHEPHERD

I'll not want.
He makes me lie in pastures green.
He leads me by the still, still waters,
his goodness restores my soul.

And I will trust in you alone.
And I will trust in you alone,
for your endless mercy follows me,
your goodness will lead me home.

(Descant)
I will trust, I will trust in you.
I will trust, I will trust in you.
Endless mercy follows me,
Goodness will lead me home.

He guides my ways in righteousness,
and he anoints my head with oil,
and my cup, it overflows with joy,
I feast on his pure delights.

And though I walk the darkest path,
I will not fear the evil one,
for you are with me, and your rod and staff
are the comfort I need to know.

Stuart Townend
Copyright © 1996 Kingsway's Thankyou Music

407
THE PRICE IS PAID

come let us enter in
to all that Jesus died
to make our own.
For every sin more than enough he gave,
and bought our freedom
from each guilty stain.

The price is paid, alleluia,
amazing grace, so strong and sure;
and so with all my heart,
my life in every part,
I live to thank you for the price you paid.

The price is paid,
see Satan flee away;
for Jesus crucified destroys his power.
No more to pay,
let accusation cease,
in Christ there is no condemnation now.

The price is paid,
and by that scourging cruel
he took our sicknesses as if his own.
And by his wounds,
his body broken there,
his healing touch may now
by faith be known.

The price is paid,
'Worthy the Lamb' we cry,
eternity shall never cease his praise.
The church of Christ
shall rule upon the earth,
in Jesus' name we have authority.

Graham Kendrick
Copyright © 1983 Kingsway's Thankyou Music

408
THE SPIRIT OF THE SOVEREIGN LORD

is upon you, because he has anointed you
to preach good news.
(Repeat)

(Men)   He has sent you to the poor,
(Women) this is the year:
(Men)   to bind up the brokenhearted,
(Women) this is the day;
(Men)   to bring freedom to the captives,
(Women) this is the year:
(All)   and to release the ones in darkness.

This is the year of the favour of the Lord.
This is the day of the vengeance of our God.
(Repeat)

The Spirit of the Sovereign Lord is upon us,
because he has anointed us
to preach good news.
(Repeat)

(Men)   He will comfort all who mourn
(Women) this is the year:
(Men)   he will provide for those who grieve;
(Women) this is the day:
(Men)   he will pour out the oil of gladness,
(Women) this is the year:
(All)   instead of mourning you will praise.

This is the year of the favour of the Lord.
This is the day of the vengeance of our God.
(Repeat)

Andy Park. Copyright © 1992
Mercy/Vineyard Publishing admin. by CopyCare

409
THE SPIRIT LIVES TO SET US FREE
walk, walk in the light.
He binds us all in unity,
walk, walk in the light.

Walk in the light,
walk in the light,
walk in the light,
walk in the light of the Lord.

Jesus promised life to all,
walk, walk in the light.
The dead were wakened by his call,
walk, walk in the light.

He died in pain on Calvary,
walk, walk in the light.
to save the lost like you and me,
walk, walk in the light.

We know his death is not the end,
walk, walk in the light.
He gave his Spirit to be our friend
walk, walk in the light.

By Jesus' love our wounds are healed,
walk, walk in the light.
The Father's kindness is revealed,
walk, walk in the light.

The Spirit lives in you and me,
walk, walk in the light.
His light will shine for all to see,
walk, walk in the light.

Damian Lundy
Copyright © 1978, 1993 Kevin Mayhew Ltd.

410
THE STEADFAST LOVE
of the Lord never ceases,
his mercies never come to an end;
they are new every morning,
new every morning,
great is thy faithfulness, O Lord,
great is thy faithfulness.

Edith McNeil. Copyright © 1974, 1975
Celebration/Kingsway's Thankyou Music

411
THE WORLD IS LOOKING FOR A HERO
we know the greatest one of all:
the mighty ruler of the nations,
King of kings and Lord of lords;
who took the nature of a servant,
and gave his life to save us all.

We will raise a shout,
we will shout it out,
he is the champion of the world.
We will raise a shout,
we will shout it out,
he is the champion of the world.

The Lord Almighty is our hero,
he breaks the stranglehold of sin.
Through Jesus' love we fear no evil;
powers of darkness flee from him.
His light will shine in every nation,
a sword of justice he will bring.

Noel & Tricia Richards
Copyright © 1994 Kingsway's Thankyou Music

411a   The suffering servant
Isaiah 53:11-12

After the suffering of his soul,
he will see the light of life and be satisfied;
by his knowledge my righteous servant will
justify many, and he will bear their iniquities.
Therefore I will give him
    a portion among the great,
and he will divide the spoils with the strong,
because he poured out his life unto death,
and was numbered with the transgressors.
For he bore the sin of many,
and made intercession for the transgressors.

412

THE TRUMPETS SOUND

the angels sing, the feast is ready to begin;
the gates of heaven are open wide,
and Jesus welcomes you inside.

Tables are laden with good things,
O taste the peace and joy he brings;
he'll fill you up with love divine,
he'll turn your water into wine.

Sing with thankfulness songs of pure delight.
Come and revel in heaven's love and light;
take your place at the table of the King.
The feast is ready to begin.
The feast is ready to begin.

The hungry heart he satisfies,
offers the poor his paradise;
now hear all heaven
and earth applaud
the amazing goodness of the Lord.

Sing with thankfulness...

Leader: Jesus,   (All echo each line)
          we thank you
          for your love,
          for your joy.
          Jesus,
          we thank you
          for the good things
          you give to us.

Sing with thankfulness...

Graham Kendrick
Copyright © 1989 Make Way Music

412a   The coming of the Lord
1 Thessalonians 4:16-18

The Lord himself will come down from
heaven, with a loud command, with the voice
of the archangel and with the trumpet call of
God, and the dead in Christ will rise first.
After that, we who are still alive and are
left will be caught up together with them
in the clouds to meet the Lord in the air.
And so we will be with the Lord for ever.
Therefore encourage each other with these
words.

413

THERE IS A REDEEMER

Jesus, God's own Son,
precious Lamb of God, Messiah,
holy One.

Thank you, O my Father,
for giving us your Son,
and leaving your Spirit
till the work on earth is done.

Jesus my Redeemer,
name above all names,
precious Lamb of God, Messiah,
O for sinners slain.

When I stand in glory
I will see his face,
and there I'll serve my King forever
in that holy place.

Melody Green. Copyright © 1982 Birdwing Music/Ears to Hear Music/
BMG Songs Inc/EMI Christian Music Publishing admin. by CopyCare

---

414

THERE IS A LOUDER SHOUT TO COME

there is a sweeter song to hear;
all the nations with one voice,
all the people with one fear.
Bowing down before your throne,
every tribe and tongue will be;
all the nations with one voice,
all the people with one King.
And what a song we'll sing upon that day.

O what a song we'll sing and
O what a tune we'll bear;
you deserve an anthem of the highest praise.
O what a joy will rise and
O what a sound we'll make;
you deserve an anthem of the highest praise.

Now we see a part of this,
one day we shall see in full;
all the nations with one voice,
all the people with one love.
No one else will share your praise,
nothing else can take your place;
all the nations with one voice,
all the people with one Lord.
And what a song we'll sing upon that day.

Even now upon the earth
there's a glimpse of all to come;
many people with one voice,
harmony of many tongues.
We will all confess your name,
you will be our only praise;
all the nations with one voice,
all the people with one God.
And what a song we'll sing upon that day.

Matt Redman
Copyright © 1996 Kingsway's Thankyou Music

415
THERE IS A VOICE
that must be heard,
there is a song that must be sung;
there is a name that must be lifted high.
There is a treasure more than gold,
there is a King upon the throne;
there is one whose praise will fill the skies.

His name is Jesus,
friend of sinners,
Jesus, Jesus,
friend of mine.

There is a peace that calms our fears,
there is a love stronger than death;
there is a hope that goes beyond the grave.
There is a friend who won't let go,
there is a heart that beats for you;
there is one name by which we are saved.

When I was captive to my fears,
you were the one who came to me,
you set me free.

Paul Oakley
Copyright © 1998 Kingsway's Thankyou Music

416
THERE IS NONE LIKE YOU
no one else can touch my heart like you do.
I could search for all eternity long
and find there is none like you.

Your mercy flows
like a river wide,
and healing comes from your hands.
Suffering children
are safe in your arms;
there is none like you.

Lenny LeBlanc. Copyright © 1991 Integrity's Hosanna! Music/
Adm. by Kingsway's Thankyou Music

416a Wisdom of God
Proverbs 3:13-15

Blessed is the man who finds wisdom,
the man who gains understanding,
for she is more profitable than silver
and yields better returns than gold.
She is more precious than rubies;
nothing you desire can compare with her.

417
THERE IS POWER IN THE NAME OF JESUS
we believe in his name.
We have called on the name of Jesus;
we are saved! We are saved!
At his name the demons flee.
At his name captives are freed.
For there is no other name that is higher
than Jesus!

There is power in the name of Jesus,
like a sword in our hands.
We declare in the name of Jesus,
we shall stand! We shall stand!
At his name God's enemies
shall be crushed beneath our feet.
For there is no other name that is higher
than Jesus!

Noel Richards
Copyright © 1989 Kingsway's Thankyou Music

418
THERE'S A PLACE
where the streets shine
with the glory of the Lamb.
There's a way, we can go there,
we can live there beyond time.

Because of you, because of you,
because of your love,
because of your blood.

No more pain, no more sadness,
no more suffering, no more tears.
No more sin, no more sickness,
no injustice, no more death.

Because of you, because of you,
because of your love,
because of your blood.

All our sins are washed away,
and we can live forever,
now we have this hope,
because of you.
Oh, we'll see you face to face,
and we will dance together
in the city of our God,
because of you.

There is joy everlasting,
there is gladness, there is peace.
There is wine ever flowing,
there's a wedding, there's a feast.

Paul Oakley
Copyright © 1995 Kingsway's Thankyou Music

419
THERE'S A SOUND ON THE WIND
like a victory song,
listen now, let it rest on your soul.
It's a song that I learned from a heavenly King,
it's the song of a battle royal.

There's a loud shout of victory
that leaps from our hearts
as we wait for our conquering King.
There's a triumph resounding from dark ages past
to the victory song we now sing.

Come on heaven's children,
the city is in sight.
There will be no sadness
on the other side.

There'll be crowns for the conquerors
and white robes to wear,
there will be no more sorrow or pain.
And the battles of earth shall be lost in the sight
of the glorious Lamb that was slain.

Now the King of the ages approaches the earth,
he will burst through the gates of the sky,
and all men shall bow down to his beautiful name,
we shall rise with a shout, we shall fly!

Come on, heaven's children,
the city is in sight.
There will be no sadness
on the other side.

Now the King of the ages approaches the earth,
he will burst through the gates of the sky,
and all men shall bow down to his beautiful name
we shall rise with a shout, we shall fly!

Graham Kendrick
Copyright © 1978 Kingsway's Thankyou Music

420
THERE'S A WIDENESS IN GOD'S MERCY
that is wider than the greatest sea;
and so I know it covers even me.
There's a depth to his compassion
that is deeper than I'll understand;
and so my life is safe within his hands.

His love is deep enough for me,
to cause these blinded eyes to see,
to set this lowly captive free from sin.
His grace is flowing from above,
reflected in the Saviour's love –
O precious Father, help me take it in.

Geoff Baker (after P.W. Faber)
Copyright © 1994 Sovereign Music UK

421
THERE'S A WIND A-BLOWING
all across the land;
fragrant breeze of heaven
blowing once again.
Don't know where it comes from,
don't know where it goes,
but let it blow over me.
Oh, sweet wind, come and blow over me.

There's a rain a-pouring,
showers from above;
mercy drops are coming,
mercy drops of love.
Turn your face to heaven,
let the water pour,
well, let it pour over me.
Oh, sweet rain, come and pour over me.

There's a fire burning,
falling from the sky;
awesome tongues of fire,
consuming you and I.
Can you feel it burning,
burn the sacrifice?
Well, let it burn over me.
Oh, sweet fire, come and burn over me.

David Ruis. Copyright © 1994
Mercy/Vineyard Publishing/ Adm. by CopyCare

422
THESE ARE THE DAYS OF ELIJAH
declaring the word of the Lord:
and these are the days of your servant Moses,
righteousness being restored.
And though these are days of great trial,
of famine and darkness and sword,
still we are a voice in the desert crying
'Prepare ye the way of the Lord.'

Behold he comes riding on the clouds,
shining like the sun at the trumpet call;
lift your voice, it's the year of jubilee,
out of Zion's hill salvation comes.

These are the days of Ezekiel,
the dry bones becoming as flesh;
and these are the days of your servant David,
rebuilding the temple of praise.
These are the days of the harvest,
the fields are as white in the world,
and we are the labourers in the vineyard,
declaring the word of the Lord.

Robin Mark
Copyright © 1997 Daybreak Music Ltd

423

THEREFORE THE REDEEMED

of the Lord shall return
and come with singing unto Zion,
and everlasting joy
shall be upon their head.

(Repeat)

They shall obtain gladness and joy,
and sorrow and mourning shall flee away.

Therefore the redeemed
of the Lord shall return
and come with singing unto Zion,
and everlasting joy
shall be upon their head.

Ruth Lake. Copyright © 1972 Scripture in Song,
a division of Integrity Music/Adm. by Kingsway's Thankyou Music

424

THINE BE THE GLORY

risen, conquering Son;
endless is the victory
thou o'er death hast won.
Angels in bright raiment
rolled the stone away,
kept the folded grave-clothes
where thy body lay.

Thine be the glory,
risen, conquering Son;
endless is the victory
thou o'er death hast won!

Lo, Jesus meets us,
risen from the tomb!
Lovingly he greets us,
scatters fear and gloom.
Let the church with gladness
hymns of triumph sing,
for her Lord now liveth,
death hath lost its sting.

No more we doubt thee,
glorious Prince of life;
life is naught without thee:
aid us in our strife;
make us more than conquerors,
through thy deathless love;
lead us in thy triumph
to thy home above.

Edmond Louis Burdy (1854-1932)
Tr. Richard Birch Hoyle (1875-1939)

425

THIS EARTH BELONGS TO GOD

the world, its wealth, and all its people;
he formed the waters wide
and fashioned every sea and shore.
Who may go up the hill of the Lord
and stand in the place of holiness?
Only the one whose heart is pure,
whose hands and lips are clean.

Lift high your heads, you gates,
rise up, you everlasting doors,
as here now the King of glory
enters into full command.
Who is the King, this King of glory,
where is the throne he comes to claim?
Christ is the King, the Lord of glory,
fresh from his victory.

Lift high your heads, you gates,
and fling wide open the ancient doors,
for here comes the King of glory
taking universal power.
Who is the King, this King of glory,
what is the power by which he reigns?
Christ is the King, his cross of glory,
and by love he rules.

All glory be to God
the Father, Son and Holy Spirit;
from ages past it was,
is now, and ever more shall be.

Christopher Idle
Words copyright © Christopher Idle/Jubilate Hymns

426

THIS IS MY DESIRE

to honour you:
Lord, with all my heart
I worship you.
All I have within me,
I give you praise:
all that I adore is in you.

Lord, I give you my heart
I give you my soul;
I live for you alone.
Ev'ry breath that I take,
ev'ry moment I'm awake;
Lord, have your way in me.

Reuben Morgan. Copyright © 1995 Reuben Morgan/
Hillsong Publishing/Kingsway's Thankyou Music

426a Love
1 Corinthians 13:1-8

And now I will show you the most excellent
way. If I speak in the tongues of men and
of angels, but have not love, I am only
a resounding gong or a clanging cymbal.
If I have the gift of prophecy and can
fathom all mysteries and all knowledge,
and if I have a faith that can move
mountains, but have not love, I am nothing.
If I give all I possess to the poor and surrender
my body to the flames, but have not love,
I gain nothing.

Love is patient, love is kind. It does not
envy, it does not boast, it is not proud.
It is not rude, it is not self-seeking, it is not
easily angered, it keeps no record of wrongs.
Love does not delight in evil but rejoices with
the truth. It always protects, always trusts,
always hopes, always perseveres.

Love never fails.

427
THIS IS THE DAY
this is the day
that the Lord has made, that the Lord has made;
we shall rejoice, we shall rejoice
and be glad in it, and be glad in it.
This is the day that the Lord has made,
we shall rejoice and be glad in it;
this is the day, this is the day
that the Lord has made.

Les Garrett. Copyright © 1967, 1980 Scripture in Song,
a division of Integrity Music/Kingsway's Thankyou Music

428
THIS IS THE PLACE
where dreams are found,
where vision comes,
called holy ground.

Holy ground,
I'm standing on holy ground,
for the Lord my God
is here with me.

Your fire burns,
but never dies;
I realise
this is holy ground.

The great I AM,

revealed to man;
take off your shoes,
this is holy ground.

Dave Bilbrough
Copyright © 1997 Kingsway's Thankyou Music

429
THOU ART WORTHY
thou art worthy, thou art worthy, O Lord.
To receive glory, glory and honour,
glory and honour and power.
For thou hast created, hast all things created,
thou hast created all things;
and for thy pleasure they are created,
thou art worthy, O Lord.

Pauline Michael Mills. Copyright © 1963, 1975
Fred Bock Music Co./Kingsway's Thankyou Music

430
THROUGH OUR GOD
WE SHALL DO VALIANTLY
it is he who will tread down our enemies.
We'll sing and shout his victory,
Christ is King!

(Last time only)
Christ is King! Christ is King!

For God has won the victory
and set his people free;
his word has slain the enemy,
the earth shall stand and see that –

Through our God...

Dale Garratt. Copyright © 1979 Scripture in Song,
a division of Integrity Music/Kingsway's Thankyou Music

431
THY WORD
is a lamp unto my feet
and a light unto my path.
(Repeat)

When I feel afraid, think I've lost my way,
still you're there right beside me.
And nothing will I fear as long as you are near;
please be near me to the end.

I will not forget your love for me, and yet
my heart forever is wandering.
Jesus, be my guide and hold me to your side,
and I will love you to the end.

Amy Grant & Michael W. Smith. Copyright © Word Music
Meadowgreen Music/EMI Christian Music Publishing adm. CopyCare

432

TO BE IN YOUR PRESENCE

to sit at your feet,
where your love surrounds me,
and makes me complete.

This is my desire, O Lord,
this is my desire.
(Repeat)

To rest in your presence,
not rushing away;
to cherish each moment,
here I would stay.

433

TO GOD BE THE GLORY!

Great things he hath done!
So loved he the world that he gave us his Son,
who yielded his life an atonement for sin,
and opened the life-gate that all may go in.

Praise the Lord! Praise the Lord!
Let the earth hear his voice!
Praise the Lord! Praise the Lord!
Let the people rejoice!
O come to the Father through Jesus the Son;
and give him the glory, great things he hath done!

O perfect redemption, the purchase of blood!
To every believer the promise of God;
the vilest offender who truly believes,
that moment from Jesus a pardon receives.

Great things he hath taught us,
great things he hath done,
and great our rejoicing through Jesus the Son:
but purer and higher and greater will be
our wonder, our worship, when Jesus we see!

434

TO YOU, O LORD

I lift up my soul, in you I trust, O my God.
Do not let me be put to shame,
nor let my enemies triumph over me.

No-one whose hope is in you
will ever be put to shame;
that's why my eyes are on you, O Lord.
Surround me, defend me,
O how I need you.
To you I lift up my soul,
to you I lift up my soul.

Show me your ways and teach me your paths,
guide me in truth, lead me on;
for you're my God, you are my Saviour,
my hope is in you each moment of the day.

No-one whose hope is in you...

Remember, Lord, your mercy and love
that ever flow from of old.
Remember not the sins of my youth
or my rebellious ways.

According to your love, remember me,
according to your love, for you are good, O Lord.

No-one whose hope is in you...

435

TO YOUR MAJESTY

and your beauty I surrender.
To your holiness and your love I surrender.
For you are an awesome God who is mighty,
you deserve my deepest praise;
with all of my heart, with all of my life I surrender.

435a Saviour of the world (a canticle)

1 Jesus, Saviour of the world,
    come to us in your mercy:
we look to you to save and help us.

2 By your cross and your life laid down,
    you set your people free:
we look to you to save and help us.

3 When they were ready to perish,
    you saved your disciples:
we look to you to come to our help.

4 In the greatness of your mercy,
    loose us from our chains,
forgive the sins of all your people.

5 Make yourself known as our Saviour
    and mighty deliverer;
save and help us that we may praise you.

6 Come now and dwell with us,
    Lord Christ Jesus:
hear our prayer and be with us always.

7 And when you come in your glory:
make us to be one with you
    and to share the life of your kingdom.

436
WAKE UP, O SLEEPER
and rise from the dead,
and Christ will shine on you.
Wake up, O sleeper
and rise from the dead,
and Christ will shine on you.

Once you were darkness
but now you are light
now you are light in the Lord.
So, as true children of light,
you must live showing the glory of God.

This is the beautiful
fruit of the light,
the good, the righteous, the true:
let us discover what pleases the Lord,
in everything that we do.

As days get darker,
take care how you live:
not as unwise but as wise;
making the most of each moment he gives,
and pressing on for the prize.

Graham Kendrick
Copyright © 1993 Make Way Music

436a   Faith in action
James 2:17

In the same way, faith by itself,
if it is not accompanied by action, is dead.

437
WE ARE A CHOSEN PEOPLE
a royal priesthood,
a holy nation,
belonging to God.
We are a chosen people,
a royal priesthood,
a holy nation,
belonging to God.

You have called us out of darkness
to declare your praise.
We exalt you and enthrone you,
glorify your name.

You have placed us into Zion
in the new Jerusalem.
Thousand thousand are their voices,
singing to the Lamb.

David J. Hadden. Copyright © 1982
Word's Spirit of Praise Music admin. by CopyCare

438
WE ARE MARCHING
in the light of God,
we are marching in the light of God.
(Repeat)

We are marching, marching,
we are marching, marching,
we are marching in the light of God.
(Repeat)

We are living in the love of God...

We are moving in the power of God...

Siyahamb' ekukhanyeni' kwenkhos'
Siyahamb' ekukhanyeni' kwenkhos'
Siyahamb' ekukhanyeni' kwenkhos'
Siyahamb' ekukhanyeni' kwenkhos'
    (khanyeni kwenkhos).

Siyahamba, (hamba, siyahamba, hamba,) - Oo
siyahamb' ekukhanyeni' kwenkhos';
    (khanyeni kwenkhos)
Siyahamba, (hamba, siyahamba, hamba,) - Oo
siyahamb' ekukhanyeni' kwenkhos';
    (khanyeni kwenkhos)

Tr. Anders Nyberg
Copyright © 1990 WGRG, Iona Community

439
WE ARE HERE TO PRAISE YOU
lift our hearts and sing.
We are here to give you
the best that we can bring.

And it is our love
rising from our hearts,
everything within us cries:
'Abba Father.'

Help us now to give you
pleasure and delight,
heart and mind and will that say:
'I love you Lord.'

Graham Kendrick
Copyright © 1985 Kingsway's Thankyou Music

439a   A worshipping people
1 Peter 2:9

But you are a chosen people,
a royal priesthood, a holy nation, a
people belonging to God, that you may
declare the praises of him who called you
out of darkness into his wonderful light.

440
WE ARE HIS CHILDREN,
the fruit of his suff'ring,
saved and redeemed by his blood.
Called to be holy, a light to the nations;
clothed with his pow'r, filled with his love.

Go forth in his name, proclaiming 'Jesus reigns!'
Now is the time for the church to arise
and proclaim him,
'Jesus, Saviour, Redeemer and Lord'
(Repeat)

Countless the souls
that are stumbling in darkness,
why do we sleep in the light?
Jesus commands us to go make disciples,
this is our cause, this is the fight.

Listen, the wind of the Spirit is blowing,
the end of the age is so near.
Pow'rs in the earth
and the heavens are shaking,
Jesus our Lord soon shall appear.

Graham Kendrick
Copyright © 1990 Make Way Music

441
WE BELIEVE
in God the Father, maker of the universe,
and in Christ his Son our Saviour,
come to us by virgin birth.
We believe he died to save us,
bore our sins, was crucified.
Then from death he rose victorious,
ascended to the Father's side.

Jesus, Lord of all, Lord of all,
Jesus, Lord of all, Lord of all,
Jesus, Lord of all, Lord of all,
Jesus, Lord of all, Lord of all.
Name above all names,
name above all names.

(Last time only)
Name above all names.

We believe he sends his Spirit,
on his church with gifts of power.
God his word of truth affirming,
sends us to the nations now.
He will come again in glory,
judge the living and the dead.
Every knee shall bow before him,
then must every tongue confess.

Graham Kendrick
Copyright © 1986 Kingsway's Thankyou Music

442
WE BOW DOWN
and confess you are Lord in this place.
We bow down and confess
you are Lord in this place.
You are all I need; it's your face I seek.
in the presence of your light
we bow down, we bow down.

Viola Grafstrom
Copyright © 1996 Kingsway's Thankyou Music

443
WE BRING THE SACRIFICE OF PRAISE
into the house of the Lord,
we bring the sacrifice of praise
into the house of the Lord.
(Repeat)

And we offer up to you
the sacrifices of thanksgiving,
and we offer up to you
the sacrifices of joy.

Kirk Dearman
Copyright © 1981 Stamps Baxter Music

444
WE DECLARE YOUR MAJESTY
we proclaim that your name is exalted;
for you reign magnificently, rule victoriously,
and your power is shown throughout the earth.
And we exclaim our God is mighty,
lift up your name, for you are holy.
Sing it again, all honour and glory,
in adoration we bow before your throne.

Malcolm du Plessis
Copyright © 1984 Kingsway's Thankyou Music

445
WE REALLY WANT TO THANK YOU, LORD
we really want to bless your name,
hallelujah! Jesus is our King!
(Repeat)

We thank you, Lord, for your gift to us,
your life so rich beyond compare,
the gift of your body here on earth
of which we sing and share.

We thank you, Lord, for our life together,
to live and move in the love of Christ,
tenderness which sets us free
to serve you with our lives.

Ed Baggett. Copyright © 1974, 1975
Celebration/Kingsway's Thankyou Music

446

WE HAVE SUNG SONGS OF VICTORY

we have prayed to you for rain;
we have cried for your compassion
to renew the land again.
Now we're standing in your presence,
more hungry than before;
now we're on your steps of mercy,
and we're knocking at your door.

How long before you drench the barren land?
How long before we see your righteous hand?
How long before your name is lifted high?
How long before the weeping turns to songs of joy?

Lord, we know your heart is broken
by the evil that you see,
and you've stayed your hand of judgement
for you plan to set men free.
But the land is still in darkness,
and we've fled from what is right;
we have failed the silent children
who will never see the light.

But I know a day is coming
when the deaf will hear his voice,
when the blind will see their Saviour,
and the lame will leap for joy.
when the widow finds a husband
who will always love his bride,
and the orphan finds a father
who will never leave her side.

How long before your glory lights the skies?
How long before your radiance lifts our eyes?
How long before your fragrance fills the air?
How long before the earth resounds with songs of joy?

447

WE KNOW THAT ALL THINGS

work together for our good,
for good to those who love the Lord;
for God has called us to be just like his Son,
to live and walk according to his word.

We are more than conquerors,
we are more than conquerors,
we are more than conquerors,
through Christ, through Christ.

I am persuaded that neither death nor life,
nor angels, principalities, nor powers,
nor things that are now,
        nor things that are to come,
can separate us from the love of Christ.

If God is for us, who against us can prevail?
No one can bring a charge against his chosen ones;
and there will be no separation from our Lord,
he has justified us through his precious blood.

448

WE SHALL STAND

with our feet on the Rock.
Whatever men may say,
we'll lift your name up high.
And we shall walk through the darkest night.
Setting our faces like flint;
we'll walk into the light.

Lord, you have chosen me for fruitfulness,
to be transformed into your likeness.
I'm gonna fight on through
till I see you face to face.

Lord, as your witnesses
you've appointed us.
And with your Holy Spirit anointed us.
And so I'll fight on through,
till I see you face to face.

449

WE SING YOUR MERCIES

we sing your endless praises,
we sing your everlasting love.
We sing your mercies, we sing your endless praises,
Sovereign One who died,
Sovereign One who died for us.

Should he who made the stars
be hung upon a tree?
And should the hands that healed
be driven through for me?
Should he who gave us bread
be made to swallow gall?
Should he who gave us breath and life
be slaughtered for us all?

Should he who is the Light
be cast into the dark?
And should the Lord of love
be pierced through his own heart?
Should he who called us friends
be deserted by us all?
Should he who lived a sinless life
be punished for our fall?

450
WE WANT TO SEE JESUS LIFTED HIGH
a banner that flies across this land,
that all men might see the truth and know
he is the way to heaven.
(Repeat)

We want to see, we want to see,
we want to see Jesus lifted high.
We want to see, we want to see,
we want to see Jesus lifted high.

Step by step we're moving forward,
little by little taking ground,
every prayer a powerful weapon,
strongholds come tumbling down,
and down, and down, and down.

We want to see Jesus lifted high...

We're gonna see, we're gonna see,
we're gonna see Jesus lifted high.
We're gonna see, we're gonna see,
we're gonna see Jesus lifted high.

Doug Horley
Copyright © 1993 Kingsway's Thankyou Music

451
WE WILL GIVE OURSELVES NO REST
till your kingdom comes on earth;
you've positioned watchmen on the walls.
Now our prayers will flow like tears,
for you've shared your heart with us;
God of heaven, on our knees we fall.

Come down in power,
reveal your heart again;
come hear our cries,
the tears that plead for rain.

We're knocking, knocking
on the door of heaven,
we're crying, crying for this generation;
we're praying for your name
to be known in all of the earth.
We're watching, watching
on the walls to see you,
we're looking, looking
for a time of breakthrough;
we're praying for your word to bear fruit
in all of the earth,
in all of the earth.

Steve Cantellow & Matt Redman
Copyright © 1996 Kingsway's Thankyou Music

452
WE WILL SEEK YOUR FACE
Almighty God,
turn and pray for you to heal our land.
Father, let revival start in us,
then every heart will know your kingdom come.

Lifting up the name of the Lord
in power and in unity,
we will see the nations turn,
touching heaven, changing earth. (x2)

Never looking back, we'll run the race;
giving you our lives, we'll gain the prize.
We will take the harvest given us
though we sow in tears, we'll reap in joy.

Lifting up...

Send revival (x2)
send revival to us.
(Repeat)

Lifting up...

... touching heaven, changing earth.

Reuben Morgan. Copyright © 1997 Reuben Morgan/
Hillsong Publishing/Kingsway's Thankyou Music

452a   Make your name known
Isaiah 64:1-2

Oh, that you would rend the heavens and
come down, that the mountains would
tremble before you!
As when fire sets twigs ablaze and causes
water to boil, come down to make your name
known to your enemies and cause the nations
to quake before you!

453
WELCOME, KING OF KINGS!
How great is your name.
You come in majesty
forever to reign.

You rule the nations,
they shake at the sound of your name.
To you is given all power,
and you shall reign.

Let all creation bow down
at the sound of your name.
Let every tongue now confess,
the Lord God reigns.

Noel Richards
Copyright © 1991 Kingsway's Thankyou Music

454
WE'LL WALK THE LAND

with hearts on fire,
and every step will be a prayer.
Hope is rising, new day dawning,
sound of singing fills the air.

Two thousand years, and still the flame
is burning bright across the land.
Hearts are waiting, longing, aching,
for awakening once again.

Let the flame burn brighter
in the heart of the darkness,
turning night to glorious day.
Let the song grow louder
as our love grows stronger,
let it shine! Let it shine!

We'll walk for truth, speak out for love;
in Jesus' name we shall be strong,
to lift the fallen, to save the children,
to fill the nation with your song.

Graham Kendrick
Copyright © 1989 Make Way Music

455
WE'RE LOOKING TO YOUR PROMISE

of old, that if we pray and humble ourselves,
you will come and heal our land,
you will come, you will come.
We're looking to the promise you made,
that if we turn and look to your face,
you will come and heal our land,
you will come, you will come to us.

Lord, send revival, start with me.
For I am one of unclean lips,
and my eyes have seen the King;
your glory I have glimpsed.
Send revival, start with me.

Matt Redman
Copyright © 1996 Kingsway's Thankyou Music

455a   The kingdom of
heaven grows
Matthew 13:31-32

He told them another parable: 'The kingdom
of heaven is like a mustard seed, which
a man took and planted in his field.
Though it is the smallest of all your seeds,
yet when it grows, it is the largest of garden
plants and becomes a tree, so that the birds of
the air come and perch in its branches.'

456
WELL, I HEAR THEY'RE SINGING

in the streets that Jesus is alive,
and all creation shouts aloud that Jesus is alive.
Now surely we can all be changed
'cause Jesus is alive;
and everybody here can know that Jesus is alive.

And I will live for all my days
to raise a banner of truth and light,
to sing about my Saviour's love
and the best thing that happened,
it was the day I met you.

I've found Jesus. (Repeat x3)

Well, I feel like dancing in the streets
'cause Jesus is alive,
to join with all who celebrate that Jesus is alive.
The joy of God is in this town
'cause Jesus is alive;
for everybody's seen the truth that Jesus is alive.

And I will live for all my days...

Well, you lifted me from where I was,
set my feet upon a rock,
humbled that you even know about me.
Now I have chosen to believe,
believing that you've chosen me;
I was lost but now I've found...

Martin Smith. Copyright © 1994 Curious? Music UK/
Adm. by Kingsway's Thankyou Music

456a   A trustworthy saying
1 Timothy 1:15a

Here is a trustworthy saying that deserves
full acceptance:
Christ Jesus came into the world to save
sinners.

457
WHAT A FRIEND I'VE FOUND

closer than a brother;
I have felt your touch,
more intimate than lovers.

Jesus, Jesus,
Jesus, friend forever.

What a hope I've found,
more faithful than a mother;
it would break my heart
to ever lose each other.

Martin Smith. Copyright © 1996 Curious? Music UK/
Adm. by Kingsway's Thankyou Music

458
WHAT A FRIEND WE HAVE IN JESUS

all our sins and griefs to bear;
what a privilege it is to carry
everything to God in prayer.

O what peace we often forfeit,
O what needless pain we bear,
all because we do not carry everything to God in prayer.

Have we trials and temptations,
is there trouble everywhere?
We should never, never be discouraged,
take it to the Lord in prayer.

Can we find a friend so faithful,
who will all our sorrows share?
Jesus knows our every weakness,
take it to the Lord in prayer.

(Instrumental)

Do your friends misunderstand you?
Take it to the Lord in prayer.
In his arms he'll take and shield you,
you will find some comfort there,
you're gonna find sweet comfort there.

Words: Trad. arranged by Mal Pope

459
WHAT A FRIEND WE HAVE IN JESUS

all our sins and griefs to bear!
What a privilege to carry
everything to God in prayer.
O what peace we often forfeit!
O what needless pain we bear!
All because we do not carry
everything to God in prayer.

Have we trials and temptations,
is there trouble anywhere?
We should never be discouraged,
take it to the Lord in prayer.
Can we find a friend so faithful
who will all our sorrows share?
Jesus knows our every weakness;
take it to the Lord in prayer.

Are we weak and heavy-laden,
cumbered with a load of care?
Precious Saviour, still our refuge,
take it to the Lord in prayer.
Do thy friends despise, forsake thee?
Take it to the Lord in prayer;
in his arms he'll take and shield thee,
thou wilt find a solace there.

Words: Joseph M Scriven (1819-86)

460
WHAT LOVE IS THIS

that took my place?
Instead of wrath you poured your grace on me.
What can I do but simply come and worship you?

I surrender, I surrender,
I surrender all to you.

What love is this that comes to save?
Upon that cross you bore my guilt and shame.
To you alone I give my heart, and worship you.

A greater love no man has seen.
It breaks sin's power and sets this prisoner free.
With all I have and all I am I worship you.

Dave Bilbrough
Copyright © 1999 Kingsway's Thankyou Music

461
WHAT KIND OF LOVE IS THIS

that gave itself for me?
I am the guilty one, yet I go free.
What kind of love is this, a love I've never known;
I didn't even know his name,
what kind of love is this?

What kind of man is this, that died in agony?
He who had done no wrong was crucified for me.
What kind of man is this, who laid aside his throne
that I may know the love of God?
What kind of man is this?

By grace I have been saved; it is the gift of God.
He destined me to be his son, such is his love.
No eye has ever seen, no ear has ever heard,
nor has the heart of man conceived
what kind of love is this.

Bryn & Sally Haworth
Copyright © 1983 Signalgrade/Kingsway's Thankyou Music

462
WHEN I LOOK INTO YOUR HOLINESS

when I gaze into your loveliness,
when all things that surround
become shadows in the light of you;
when I've found the joy of reaching your heart,
when my will becomes enthralled in your love,
when all things that surround
become shadows in the light of you:

I worship you, I worship you,
the reason I live is to worship you.
(Repeat)

Wayne & Cathy Perrin. Copyright © 1980
Integrity's Hosanna! Music. Adm. Kingsway's Thankyou Music

462a Doxology
Jude 24-25

To him who is able to keep you from falling
and to present you before his glorious presence
without fault and with great joy
– to the only God our Saviour
be glory, majesty, power and authority,
through Jesus Christ our Lord,
before all ages, now and for evermore!
Amen

463
WHEN I FEEL THE TOUCH
of your hand upon my life,
it causes me to sing a song
that I love you, Lord.
So from deep within
my spirit singeth unto thee,
you are my King, you are my God,
and I love you, Lord.

Keri Jones & David Matthews
Copyright © 1978 Word's Spirit of Praise Music admin. by CopyCare

464
WHEN I NEEDED A NEIGHBOUR
were you there, were you there?
When I needed a neighbour were you there?

And the creed and the colour
and the name won't matter,
were you there?

I was hungry and thirsty,
were you there, were you there?
I was hungry and thirsty, were you there?

I was cold, I was naked,
were you there, were you there?
I was cold, I was naked, were you there?

When I needed a shelter
were you there, were you there?
When I needed a shelter were you there?

When I needed a healer
were you there, were you there?
When I needed a healer were you there?

Wherever you travel I'll be there, I'll be there,
wherever you travel I'll be there.

And the creed and the colour
and the name won't matter, I'll be there.

Sydney Carter
Copyright © 1965 Stainer & Bell Ltd

465
WHEN I SURVEY
the wondrous cross
on which the Prince of glory died,
my richest gain I count but loss,
and pour contempt on all my pride.

Forbid it, Lord, that I should boast,
save in the death of Christ my God:
all the vain things that charm me most,
I sacrifice them to his blood.

See from his head, his hands, his feet,
sorrow and love flow mingled down:
did e'er such love and sorrow meet,
or thorns compose so rich a crown?

Were the whole realm of nature mine,
that were an offering far too small;
love so amazing, so divine,
demands my soul, my life, my all!

Isaac Watts (1674-1748)

466
WHEN I SURVEY
the wondrous cross
on which the Prince of glory died,
my richest gain I count but loss,
and pour contempt on all my pride.

Forbid it, Lord, that I should boast,
save in the death of Christ my God:
all the vain things that charm me most,
I sacrifice them to his blood.

See from his head, his hands, his feet,
sorrow and love flow mingled down:
did e'er such love and sorrow meet,
or thorns compose so rich a crown?

Were the whole realm of nature mine,
that were an offering far too small;
love so amazing, so divine,
demands my soul, my life, my all!

Isaac Watts (1674-1748)

467
WHEN THE MUSIC FADES
all is stripped away,
and I simply come;
longing just to bring something that's of worth
that will bless your heart.

I'll bring you more than a song,
for a song in itself
is not what you have required.

You search much deeper within
through the way things appear;
you're looking into my heart.

I'm coming back to the heart of worship
and it's all about you, all about you, Jesus.
I'm sorry, Lord, for the thing I've made it,
when it's all about you, all about you, Jesus.

King of endless worth,
no one could express
how much you deserve.
Though I'm weak and poor,
all I have is yours, every single breath.

Matt Redman
Copyright © 1997 Kingsway's Thankyou Music

468
WHERE THERE ONCE WAS ONLY HURT
he gave his healing hand;
where there once was only pain,
he brought comfort like a friend.
I feel the sweetness of his love
piercing my darkness.
I see the bright and morning sun
as it ushers in his joyful gladness.

He's turned my mourning into dancing again,
he's lifted my sorrow.
I can't stay silent, I must sing
for his joy has come.

His anger lasts for a moment in time;
but his favour is here
and will be on me for all my lifetime.

Tommy Walker. Copyright © 1992 Integrity's Hosanna! Music/
Adm. by Kingsway's Thankyou Music

469
WHO CAN SOUND
THE DEPTHS OF SORROW
in the father heart of God,
for the children we've rejected,
for the lives so deeply scarred?
And each light that we've extinguished
has brought darkness to our land:
upon our nation, upon our nation,
have mercy, Lord.

We have scorned the truth you gave us,
we have bowed to other lords.
We have sacrificed the children
on the altars of our gods.

O let truth again shine on us,
let your holy fear descend:
upon our nation, upon our nation,
have mercy, Lord.

(Men)   Who can stand before your anger?
Who can face your piercing eyes?
For you love the weak and helpless,
and you hear the victims' cries.

(All)   Yes, you are a God of justice,
and your judgement surely comes:
upon our nation, upon our nation,
have mercy, Lord.

(Women) Who will stand against the violence?
Who will comfort those who mourn?
In an age of cruel rejection,
who will build for love a home?

(All)   Come and shake us into action,
come and melt our hearts of stone:
upon your people, upon your people,
have mercy, Lord.

Who can sound the depths of mercy
in the father heart of God?
For there is a man of sorrows
who for sinners shed his blood.
He can heal the wounds of nations,
he can wash the guilty clean:
because of Jesus, because of Jesus,
have mercy, Lord.

Graham Kendrick
Copyright © 1988 Make Way Music

470
WHO IS THERE LIKE YOU
and who else would give their life for me,
even suffering in my place?
And who could repay you?
All of creation looks to you,
and you provide for all you have made.

So I'm lifting up my hands,
lifting up my voice,
lifting up your name,
and in your grace I rest,
for your love has come to me
and set me free.

And I'm trusting in your word,
trusting in your cross,
trusting in your blood
and all your faithfulness,
for your power at work in me
is changing me.

Paul Oakley
Copyright © 1995 Kingsway's Thankyou Music

471
WHO PAINTS THE SKIES
into glorious day?
Only the splendour of Jesus.
Who breathes his life into fists of clay?
Only the splendour of Jesus.
Who shapes the valleys and brings the rain?
Only the splendour of Jesus.
Who makes the desert to live again?
Only the splendour of Jesus.

Teach every nation his marvellous ways;
each generation shall sing his praise.

He is wonderful, he is glorious,
clothed in righteousness, full of tenderness.
Come and worship him, he's the Prince of life,
he will cleanse our hearts in his river of fire.

Who hears the cry of the barren one?
Only the mercy of Jesus.
Who breaks the curse of the heart of stone?
Only the mercy of Jesus.
Who storms the prison and sets men free?
Only the mercy of Jesus.
Purchasing souls for eternity?
Only the mercy of Jesus.

Stuart Townend
Copyright © 1995 Kingsway's Thankyou Music

472
WIND, WIND, BLOW ON ME
wind, wind, set me free,
wind, wind, my Father
sent the blessèd Holy Spirit.

Jesus told us all about you,
how we could not live without you,
with his blood the power bought,
to help us live the life he taught.

When we're weary you console us;
when we're lonely you enfold us;
when in danger you uphold us,
blessèd Holy Spirit.

When unto the church you came
it was not in your own but Jesus' name.
Jesus Christ is still the same,
he sends the Holy Spirit.

Set us free to love our brothers;
set us free to live for others,
that the world the Son might see,
and Jesus' name exalted be.

Jane & Betsy Clowe. Copyright © 1974, 1975
Celebration/Kingsway's Thankyou Music

472a   Bless the Lord

1. Blessed are you, the God of our ancestors,
   worthy to be praised and exalted for ever.

2. Blessed is your holy and glorious name,
   worthy to be praised and exalted for ever.

3. Blessed are you,
      in your holy and glorious temple,
   worthy to be praised and exalted for ever.

4. Blessed are you who look into the depths,
   worthy to be praised and exalted for ever.

5. Blessed are you,
      enthroned on the cherubim,
   worthy to be praised and exalted for ever.

6. Blessed are you
      on the throne of your kingdom,
   worthy to be praised and exalted for ever.

7. Blessed are you in the heights of heaven
   worthy to be praised and exalted for ever.

Bless the Father, the Son and the Holy Spirit,
worthy to be praised and exalted for ever.

From Common Worship:
Services and Prayers for the Church of England.

473
WITH MY WHOLE HEART
I will praise you,
holding nothing back, hallelujah!
You have made me glad and now
I come with open arms to thank you,
with my heart embrace, hallelujah!
I can see your face is smiling.
With my whole life I will serve you,
captured by your love, hallelujah!
O amazing love, O amazing love!

Lord, your heart is overflowing
with a love divine, hallelujah!
And this love is mine for ever.
Now your joy has set you laughing
as you join the song, hallelujah!
Heaven sings along, I hear the
voices swell to great crescendos,
praising your great love, hallelujah!
O amazing love, O amazing love!

Come, O Bridegroom, clothed in splendour,
my belovèd one, hallelujah!
How I long to run and meet you.

You're the fairest of ten thousand,
you're my life and breath, hallelujah!
Love as strong as death has won me.
All the rivers, all the oceans
cannot quench this love, hallelujah!
O amazing love, O amazing love!

Graham Kendrick
Copyright © 1981 Kingsway's Thankyou Music

474
WITHIN THE VEIL

I now would come,
into the holy place, to look upon thy face.
I see such beauty there, no other can compare;
I worship thee, my Lord, within the veil.

Ruth Dryden. Copyright © 1978
Genesis Music/Kingsway's Thankyou Music.

475
WONDERFUL GRACE

that gives what I don't deserve,
pays me what Christ has earned,
then lets me go free.
Wonderful grace,
that gives me the time to change,
washes away the stains that once covered me.

And all that I have I lay at the feet
of the wonderful Saviour who loves me.

Wonderful grace, that held in the face of death,
breathed in its latest breath
forgiveness for me.
Wonderful love,
whose power can break every chain,
giving us life again, setting us free.

John Pantry
Copyright © 1990 HarperCollins Religious admin. by CopyCare

476
WORTHY, O WORTHY ARE YOU LORD

worthy to be thanked and praised
and worshipped and adored.
Worthy, O worthy are you Lord,
worthy to be thanked and praised
and worshipped and adored.

Singing, hallelujah, Lamb upon the throne,
we worship and adore you,
make your glory known.
Hallelujah, glory to the King:
you're more than a conqueror,
you're Lord of everything.

Mark Kinzer. Copyright © 1976
The Word of God Music admin. by CopyCare

477
YOU ARE A HOLY GOD

an all consuming fire.
You're robed in majesty
bright shining as the sun.

Your ways are not our ways
your thoughts are high above.
You are the fountain, Lord,
of mercy, truth and love.

(And we cry) Holy,
holy is the Lord God most high.
(And we cry) Holy,
holy is the Lord most high.

Brian Duane & Kathryn Scott. Copyright © 1999
Vineyard Songs (UK/Eire) admin. by CopyCare

478
YOU ARE BEAUTIFUL
BEYOND DESCRIPTION

too marvellous for words,
too wonderful for comprehension,
like nothing ever seen or heard.
Who can grasp your infinite wisdom?
Who can fathom
the depth of your love?
You are beautiful beyond description,
Majesty, enthroned above.

And I stand, I stand in awe of you.
I stand, I stand in awe of you.
Holy God, to whom all praise is due,
I stand in awe of you.

Mark Altrogge. Copyright © 1987
People of Destiny International admin. by CopyCare.

478a His glory
2 Thessalonians 1:10a

... on the day he comes to be glorified in his
holy people and to be marvelled at among all
those who have believed.

479
YOU ARE CROWNED WITH MANY CROWNS

and rule all things in righteousness.
You are crowned with many crowns,
upholding all things by your word.
You rule in power and reign in glory!
You are Lord of heaven and earth!
You are Lord of all. You are Lord of all.

John Sellers. Copyright © 1984
Integrity's Hosanna! Music. Adm. Kingsway's Thankyou Music

479a In awe of God
Ecclesiastes 5:2

Do not be quick with your mouth,
do not be hasty in your heart
to utter anything before God.
God is in heaven and you are on earth,
so let your words be few.

480
YOU ARE MERCIFUL TO ME
you are merciful to me,
you are merciful to me, my Lord.
(Repeat)

Every day my disobedience
grieves your loving heart;
but then redeeming love breaks through,
and causes me to worship you.

(Men & Women echo)
Redeemer,
Saviour,
Healer
and friend.
Every day
renew my ways,
fill me with love
that never ends.

Ian White. Copyright © 1997 Little Misty Music/
Kingsway's Thankyou Music

481
YOU ARE MIGHTY
you are holy,
you are awesome in your power.
You have risen,
you have conquered,
you have beaten the power of death.

Hallelujah, we will rejoice.
Hallelujah, we will rejoice.

Craig Musseau. Copyright © 1989
Mercy/Vineyard Publishing/ Adm. by CopyCare

481a Eternal King
Lamentations 5:19

You, O Lord, reign for ever;
your throne endures
from generation to generation.

482a The Eucharistic prayer

The Lord is here.
His Spirit is with us.
Lift up your hearts.
We lift them to the Lord.
Let us give thanks to the Lord our God.
It is right to give thanks and praise.

Father, you made the world and love your
creation. You gave your Son Jesus Christ
to be our Saviour.
His dying and rising have set us free from
sin and death. And so we gladly thank you,
with saints and angels praising you,
and saying:

Holy, holy, holy Lord,
God of power and might,
heaven and earth are full of your glory.
Hosanna in the highest.

We praise and bless you, loving Father,
through Jesus Christ, our Lord;
and as we obey his command,
send your Holy Spirit, that broken bread and
wine outpoured may be for us the body and
blood of your dear Son.

On the night before he died
he had supper with his friends
and, taking bread, he praised you.
He broke the bread, gave it to them and said:
Take, eat; this is my body which is given for
you; do this in remembrance of me.

When supper was ended he took the cup of
wine. Again he praised you, gave it to them
and said: Drink this, all of you; this is my
blood of the new covenant, which is shed
for you and for many for the forgiveness of
sins. Do this, as often as you drink it, in
remembrance of me.

So, Father, we remember all that Jesus
did, in him we plead with confidence his
sacrifice made once for all upon the cross.
Bringing before you the bread of life and
cup of salvation, we proclaim his death and
resurrection until he comes in glory.

Christ has died:
Christ is risen:
Christ will come again.

From Common Worship:
Services and Prayers for the Church of England.

482
YOU ARE MY HIDING PLACE
you always fill my heart
with songs of deliverance,
whenever I am afraid I will trust in you.
I will trust in you; let the weak say
'I am strong in the strength of my God.'

Michael Ledner. Copyright © 1981
Maranatha! Music/Adm. by CopyCare

483
YOU ARE MY PASSION
love of my life,
friend and companion, my lover.
All of my being longs for your touch;
with all my heart I love you.
Now will you draw me close to you,
gather me in your arms;
let me hear the beating of your heart,
O my Jesus, O my Jesus.

Noel & Tricia Richards
Copyright © 1995 Kingsway's Thankyou Music

483a   No-one like our God
1 Samuel 2:2

There is no-one holy like the Lord;
there is no-one besides you;
there is no Rock like our God.

484
YOU ARE THE HOLY ONE,
the Lord most high.
You reign in majesty,
you reign on high.
You are the worthy One
Lamb that was slain.
You bought us with your blood,
and with you we'll reign.

We exalt your name,
high and mighty one of Israel,
we exalt your name. Lead us on to war,
in the power of your name.
We exalt your name,
the name above all names,
our victorious King, we exalt your name.

You are the holy One,
the Lord most high.
You reign in majesty,
you reign on high.

You are the King of kings,
the Lord of lords;
all men will bow to you,
before your throne.

Andy Park. Copyright © 1988
Mercy/Vineyard Publishing admin by CopyCare

485
YOU ARE THE KING OF GLORY
you are the Prince of Peace;
you are the Lord of heaven and earth,
you're the Son of righteousness.
Angels bow down before you,
worship and adore, for
you have the words of eternal life,
you are Jesus Christ the Lord.

Hosanna to the Son of David!
Hosanna to the King of kings!
Glory in the highest heaven,
for Jesus the Messiah reigns.

Mavis Ford. Copyright © 1978
Word's Spirit of Praise Music admin. by CopyCare

486
YOU ARE THE MIGHTY KING
the living Word;
master of everything,
you are the Lord.

And I praise your name,
and I praise your name.

You are Almighty God,
Saviour and Lord;
wonderful Counsellor,
you are the Lord.

And I praise your name,
and I praise your name.

You are the Prince of Peace,
Emmanuel;
everlasting Father,
you are the Lord.

And I love your name,
and I love your name.

(Repeat verse 1)

Eddie Espinosa. Copyright © 1982
Mercy/Vineyard Publishing admin. by CopyCare

487
YOU ARE THE PERFECT
AND RIGHTEOUS GOD
whose presence bears no sin;
you bid me come to your holy place:
how can I enter in
when your presence bears no sin?
Through him who poured out his life for me,
the atoning Lamb of God,
through him and his work alone I boldly come.

I come by the blood, I come by the cross,
where your mercy flows
from hands pierced for me.
For I dare not stand on my righteousness,
my every hope rests on what Christ has done,
and I come by the blood.

You are the high and exalted King,
the one the angels fear;
so far above me in every way,
Lord, how can I draw near
to the one the angels fear?
Through him who laid down his life for me
and ascended to your side,
through him, through Jesus alone I boldly come.

Steve & Vikki Cook. Copyright © 1994
People of Destiny International/Word Music/Adm. by CopyCare

488a The Vine and the branches
John 15:5-8

'I am the vine; you are the branches.
If a man remains in me
and I in him, he will bear much fruit;
apart from me you can do nothing.
If anyone does not remain in me,
he is like a branch that is thrown away
and withers; such branches are picked up,
thrown into the fire and burned.
If you remain in me
and my words remain in you,
ask whatever you wish,
and it will be given you.
This is to my Father's glory,
that you bear much fruit,
showing yourselves to be my disciples.'

488
YOU ARE THE VINE
we are the branches,
keep us abiding in you.
You are the Vine, we are the branches,
keep us abiding in you.

Then we'll grow in your love,
then we'll go in your name,
that the world will surely know
that you have power to heal and to save.

Danny Daniels & Randy Rigby. Copyright © 1982
Mercy/Vineyard Publishing admin by CopyCare

489
YOU DID NOT WAIT FOR ME
to draw near to you,
but you clothed yourself in frail humanity.
You did not wait for me to cry out to you,
but you let me hear your voice calling me.

And I'm forever grateful to you,
I'm forever grateful for the cross;
I'm forever grateful to you,
that you came to seek and save the lost.

Mark Altrogge. Copyright © 1985
People of Destiny International admin by CopyCare

490
YOU HAVE SHOWN ME
favour unending.
You have given your life for me.
And my heart knows of your goodness,
your blood has covered me.

I will arise and give thanks to you,
Lord, my God.
And your name I will bless with my whole heart.
You have shown mercy,
you have shown mercy to me.
I give thanks to you Lord.

You have poured out your healing upon us,
you have set the captives free:
and we know it's not what we've done,
but by your hand alone.

We will arise and give thanks to you,
Lord, our God.
And your name we will bless with all our hearts.
You have shown mercy,
you have shown mercy to us.
We give thanks to you, Lord.

You, oh Lord, are the healer of my (our) soul;
you, oh Lord are the gracious Redeemer.
You come to restore us again.
Yes, you come to restore us again,
and again.

I give thanks to you, Lord.
I give thanks to you, Lord.

Brian Thiessen. Copyright © 1991
Mercy/Vineyard Publishing admin. by CopyCare

491
YOU HAVE CALLED US CHOSEN
a royal priesthood,
a holy nation, we belong to you.
(Repeat)

Take our lives as a sacrifice;
shine in us your holy light.
Purify our hearts' desire;
be to us a consuming fire.

You have shown us mercy,
you have redeemed us;
our hearts cry 'Father, we belong to you.'
(Repeat)

Andy Park. Copyright © 1991
Mercy/Vineyard Publishing admin. by CopyCare

491a   A prayer of thanksgiving

Blessed are you, Lord our God,
Creator and Redeemer of all;
to you be glory and praise for ever.
From the waters of chaos you drew
forth the world and in your great love
    fashioned us in your image.
Now, through the deep waters of death,
you have brought your people to new birth
by raising your Son to life in triumph.
May Christ your light ever dawn in our hearts
as we offer you our sacrifice
    of thanks and praise.
Blessed be God, Father, Son and Holy Spirit:

All   Blessed be God for ever.

From Common Worship:
Services and Prayers for the Church of England.

492
YOU LAID ASIDE YOUR MAJESTY
gave up everything for me,
suffered at the hands of those you had created.
You took all my guilt and shame,
when you died and rose again;
now today you reign,
in heaven and earth exalted.

I really want to worship you, my Lord,
you have won my heart and I am yours
for ever and ever; I will love you.
You are the only one who died for me,
gave your life to set me free,
so I lift my voice to you in adoration.

Noel Richards
Copyright © 1985 Kingsway's Thankyou Music

493
YOU MAKE YOUR FACE
TO SHINE ON ME
and that my soul knows very well;
you lift me up, I'm cleansed and free,
and that my soul knows very well.

When mountains fall I'll stand
by the power of your hand,
and in your heart of hearts I'll dwell,
and that my soul knows very well.
(Repeat)

Joy and strength each day I'll find,
and that my soul knows very well;
forgiveness, hope I know is mine,
and that my soul knows very well.

Darlene Zschech & Russell Fragar. Copyright © 1996 Darlene Zschech
& Russell Fragar/Hillsong Publishing/Kingsway's Thankyou Music

493a   Priestly blessing
Numbers 6:24-26

The Lord bless you and keep you,
the Lord make his face shine upon you
and be gracious to you;
the Lord turn his face towards you
and give you peace.

494
YOU, O LORD
rich in mercy,
because of your great love.
You, O Lord, so loved us,
even when we were dead in our sins.

(Men)
You made us alive
together with Christ,
and raised us up together with him,
and seated us with him in heavenly places,
and raised us up together with him,
and seated us with him in heavenly places
in Christ.

(Women)
You made us alive together with Christ,
and raised us up,
and seated us,
and raised us up,
and seated us in Christ.

Mark Veary & Paul Oakley
Copyright © 1986 Kingsway's Thankyou Music

495

YOU SHALL GO OUT WITH JOY

and be led forth with peace,
and the mountains and the hills
shall break forth before you.
There'll be shouts of joy,
and the trees of the field
shall clap, shall clap their hands.

And the trees of the field shall clap their hands,
and the trees of the field shall clap their hands,
and the trees of the field shall clap their hands,
and you'll go out with joy.

495a   The conclusion
of Night Prayer

In peace we will lie down and sleep;
for you alone, Lord, make us dwell in safety.
Abide with us, Lord Jesus,
for the night is at hand
    and the day is now past.
As the night watch looks for the morning,
so do we look for you, O Christ.
Come with the dawning of the day
and make yourself known
    in the breaking of the bread.
The Lord bless us and watch over us;
the Lord make his face shine upon us
    and be gracious to us;
the Lord look kindly on us and give us peace.
Amen

496

YOU'RE THE LION OF JUDAH

the Lamb that was slain,
you ascended to heaven and ever more will reign;
at the end of the age when the earth you reclaim,
you will gather the nations before you.

And the eyes of all men will be
fixed on the Lamb who was crucified,
for with wisdom and mercy and justice
you'll reign at your Father's side.

And the angels will cry: 'Hail the Lamb
who was slain for the world, rule in power.'
And the earth will reply: 'You shall reign
as the King of all kings and the Lord of all lords.'

There's a shield in our hand and a sword at our side,
there's a fire in our spirit that cannot be denied;
as the Father has told us, for these you have died,
for the nations that gather before you.

And the ears of all men need to hear
of the Lamb who was crucified,
who descended to hell yet was raised up
to reign at the Father's side.

And the angels will cry: 'Hail the Lamb
who was slain for the world, rule in power.'
And the earth will reply: 'You shall reign
as the King of all kings and the Lord of all lords.'

497

YOUR EYE IS ON THE SPARROW

and your hand, it comforts me.
From the ends of the earth
to the depths of my heart,
let your mercy and strength be seen.
You call me to your purpose,
as angels understand.
For your glory may you draw all men,
as your love and grace demands.

And I will run to you, to your words of truth;
not by might, not by power
            but by the Spirit of God.
Yes, I will run the race, 'till I see your face.
Oh, let me live in the glory of your grace.

498

YOUR LOVE, O LORD

It reaches to the heavens;
your faithfulness, it reaches to the skies.
Your righteousness is like
the mighty mountains;
how priceless is your faithful love.

I will exalt you, O Lord,
I will exalt you, O Lord.
Praise your holy name,
that my heart may sing to you;
I will exalt you, O Lord.

Your name, O Lord, it is a mighty tower;
your glory, it covers all the earth.
In your hands alone
are strength and power,
all praise be to your glorious name.

499
YOUR MERCY FLOWS
upon us like a river.
Your mercy stands unshakeable and true.
Most holy God, of all good things the giver,
we turn and lift our fervent prayer to you.

(Leader & echo)
Hear our cry,
O Lord,
be merciful
once more;
let your love
your anger stem,
remember mercy, O Lord, again.

Your church once great,
though standing clothed in sorrow,
is even still the bride that you adore;
revive your church, that we again may honour
our God and King, our Master and our Lord.

As we have slept, this nation has been taken
by every sin ever known to man;
so at its gates, though burnt by fire and broken,
in Jesus' name we come to take our stand.

Wes Sutton
Copyright © 1987 Sovereign Lifestyle Music

500
YOUR LOVE, SHINING LIKE THE SUN
pouring like the rain,
raging like the storm,
refreshing me again.
Ooh, I receive your love.

Your grace
frees me from the past,
it purges every sin,
it purifies my heart
and heals me from within,
ooh, I receive your grace.

Pour over me, pour over me,
let your rain flood this thirsty soul.
Pour over me your waves of love,
pour over me.

I come and lay my burden down
gladly at your feet,
I'm opening up my heart,
come make this joy complete;
ooh, I receive your peace.

Pour over me...

Stuart Townend
Copyright © 1999 Kingsway's Thankyou Music

Index of liturgy and Bible verses

Liturgy is listed in italics

*Note for information: in the Church of England the Absolution and Eucharistic prayers are only said by those who have been ordained as priests.

Index
Song titles differing from first lines are in italics

118

120

Copyright and photocopying

Acknowledgements
Scripture quotations taken from the HOLY BIBLE, NEW INTERNATIONAL VERSION.
Copyright ©1973, 1978, 1984 by International Bible Society. Used by permission of Hodder and Stoughton Limited. All rights reserved. "NIV" is a registered trade mark of International Bible Society. UK trademark number 1448790
Common Worship: Services and Prayers for the Church of England (Church House Publishing, 2000) material from which is included in this book is copyright © The Archbishops' Council 2000 and is reproduced by permission.

Layout by Spring Harvest
Cover design by Adept Design
Printed in the UK by Halcyon

Published by Spring Harvest, 14 Horsted Square, Uckfield, East Sussex, TN22 1QL, UK.
Spring Harvest. A Registered Charity.

ISBN 1 899 78835 2

Copyright Holders

Ascent Music P.O. Box 263 Croydon Surrey, CR9 5AP

Bishop Timothy Dudley Smith 9 Ashlands Ford Salisbury Wiltshire SP4 6DY

BMG Music Publishing Int. Ltd Copyright Department Bedford House 69-79 Fulham High Street London SW6 3JW

Bucks Music Ltd Onward House 11 Uxbridge Street London W8 7TQ

C Simmonds School House 81 Clapham Road Bedford MK1 7RB

Calamus 30 North Terrace Milden Hall Suffolk IP28 7AB

CopyCare P.O. Box 77 Hailsham East Sussex, BN27 3EF

David Higham Associates Ltd 5-8 Lower John Street Golden Square London W1R 4HA

Daybreak Music Ltd Silverdale Road Eastbourne East Sussex BN20 7AB

Franciscian Communications Inc 1229 South Santee Street Los Angeles CA 90015 USA

G.I.A. Publications Inc 7404 S. Mason Avenue Chicago IL 60638 USA

Harwood Settlement Public Trust Office Stewart House 24 Kingsway London WC2B 6JX

High-Fye Music Ltd 8-9 Frith Street London W1 5TZ

I.Q. Music Commercial House 52 Perrymount Road Haywards Heath West Sussex

Ironspiration Music 24 Cobbs Road Woombye Queensland 4559 Australia

J Curwin & Sons Music Sales 8-9 Frith Street London W1V 5TZ

Josef Weinberger 12-14 Mortimer Street London W1T 3JJ

Jubilate Hymns 4 Thorne Park Road Chelston Torquay TQ2 6RX

Kay Chance Glaubenszentrum Dr.-Heinrich-Jasper-Str. 20 D-37581 Bad Gandersheim Germany

Kevin Mayhew Ltd Buxhall Stowmarket Suffolk IP14 3DJ

Kingsway's Thankyou Music Lottbridge Drove Eastbourne East Sussex BN23 6NT

Make Way Music P.O. Box 263 Croydon Surrey, CR9 5AP

MCA Music Publishing 2440 Sepulveda Blvd., Suite 100 Los Angeles CA 90064-1712 USA

Mr P Hemingway 109 Spring Bank Hull North Humberside HU3 1BH

Oxford University Press Great Clarendon Street Oxford OX2 6DP

Pete Sanchez Jnr 4723 Hickory Downs Houston Texas 77084 USA

Polygram Music 347-353 Chiswick High Street Chiswick London W4 4HS

Rocksmith Music Leosong Copyright Service Ltd. Independent House 54 Larkshall Road Chingford London E4 6PD

SGO Music Publishing Unit 25 The Quadrangle 49 Atlanta Street Fulham London SW6 6TU

Sovereign Music UK PO Box 356 Leighton Buzzard Beds. LU7 8WP

Stainer & Bell Ltd P.O. Box 110 Victoria House 23 Gruneisen Road Finchley London N3 1DZ

Taize Community Ateliers et Presses de Taize F-71250 Taize Communaute France

TKO Music Publishing P.O. Box 130 Hove East Sussex BN3 6QU

Warner/Chappell Music Ltd Griffin House 161 Hammersmith Road London W6 8BS UK

Wild Goose Resource Group, Pearce Institute, 840 Govan Road, Glasgow G51 3UU

About Spring Harvest

Spring Harvest is Europe's largest annual Christian event, welcoming up to 60,000 Christians of all ages and denominations. They enjoy worship, Bible teaching, workshops and leisure activities set in high quality holiday centres.

The aim of Spring Harvest is to equip the church for action. This vision is fulfilled through a range of events, conferences, books, music albums and other resources.

For more information about Spring Harvest events and resources, contact the Customer Service team.

tel: 01825 769000
fax: 01825 769141
email: info@springharvest.org
web: www.springharvest.org